Cheesecraft

Cheesecraft

BY

RITA ASH

TABB HOUSE
11 Church Street, Padstow, Cornwall

First published in 1983
by Tabb House, 11 Church Street, Padstow, Cornwall. PL28 8BG

Copyright © Rita Ash, 1983
Drawings Copyright © Susan Cutting

Printed in Great Britain by
Century Litho (Truro) Ltd, Ashfield, Ponsharden, Falmouth, Cornwall. TR11 2SR.

Bound by R. Booth (Bookbinders) Ltd., Carnstead, Mabe, Cornwall.

MY THANKS

to Major Patrick Rance, author of *The Great British Cheese;* Mrs Olivia Mills, author of *Practical Sheep Dairying;* and the late Mrs Joan Shields, author of *practical Goat Keeping;*

to Mrs L. Roden of Bicton College, Hilary Storer, and Julia Hallett, for their advice and encouragement;

to the students who asked the questions I have endeavoured to answer, and of course to my husband for his patient, practical assistance.

Rita Ash

CONTENTS

PART TWO — CHEESES

ILLUSTRATIONS

INTRODUCTION

CHEESE CAN BE MADE successfully in the average kitchen with no more difficulty than bread or preserves. In fact, within living memory, it was made in country kitchens everywhere. Cheesemaking needs no special skills. What is needed is time, patience, and a lot of milk.

Each gallon of milk produces about one pound of cheese, so that unless you have a source of cheap milk, you will find the product expensive. With milk at, say, twenty pence per pint from the dairy, and the additional cost of the other ingredients and the heat required for the making, your cheese will cost about £1.80 per pound. You can, of course, buy cheese cheaper than this in the shops, but the pleasure of serving your own homemade cheese may make the additional cost worthwhile. If you have a house cow or a goat or a source of cheap milk, you will find cheesemaking a real saving.

Beginners may prefer to start with the soft cheeses which require only simple kitchen utensils; but almost certainly, once started, they will soon progress to the semi-hard and hard pressed cheeses which require the purchase of a few pieces of special equipment. The more successful you are, the more adventurous you can become.

The recipes and methods for making the cheeses included in this book have all been proven in the author's own kitchens and they give a variety of textures and flavours. Whether the cheeses are typical of their names is a matter of opinion. They are certainly very enjoyable, and that, surely, is the most important thing.

Cheesemaking is a simple skill. It must be. Kitchen and dairymaids had little education and knew no science, yet they managed to make excellent cheese. The very fact that you are able to read this book must make it easier for you.

PART ONE
GENERAL INFORMATION

CHAPTER ONE
PRINCIPLES

THIS BOOK does not go deeply into the science of cheesemaking; readers who wish to do so will find a number of books on the subject in the libraries of agricultural and dairying colleges. Those books are mostly concerned with large scale commercial cheesemaking and unfortunately many of them have not been recently revised. They are, however, most interesting and informative.

Cheesemaking is a practical skill far more than a science, but it is important that every cheesemaker should be aware of the basic principles. This requires a knowledge of the composition of milk and an understanding of the bacteriological and physical changes which take place during the cheesemaking process.

COWS' MILK is made up of approximately 87% water, 3½% protein, 3½-4% fat, carbohydrates — mainly lactose or milk sugar —, minerals and vitamins. Milk from certain breeds of cattle will have a higher fat and a lower water content. Milk from other animals differs again. With the goat, for example, the milk contains more protein and fat but less sugar.

Milk in its natural state is a very valuable food, but it suffers from two major drawbacks. Because of its high water content, which is of no nutritional value, it is bulky to store, and because it is so nourishing, it is very attractive to micro-organisms. When micro-organisms multiply in the milk, they feed upon the lactose or milk sugar and produce lactic acid, a procedure commonly called 'souring'. When the bacteria have produced enough acid, and the milk is sufficiently sour, the solids or 'curd' will separate from the liquid or 'whey'. This separation is caused by the effect that acid has upon the protein in the milk.

THE PROTEIN — chiefly that protein called casein — is present in untreated or 'raw' milk in a form which will not easily separate from the whey; it must first be solidified or 'coagulated'. This coagulation can be brought about by the presence of an acid, as in the case of sour milk. It can also be caused by enzyme action. The enzyme rennin is produced in the stomach of young animals in order to coagulate the suckled milk so that the water is expelled and the curd can be more slowly absorbed in the digestive system. Heat has a limited coagulating effect. If milk is boiled fiercely, a small number of particles of solidified protein will be found floating on the surface and adhering to the vessel.

FAT is present in the milk as 'globules' — the size of these particles varies in the milk of different species. This is one of the reasons why goats' milk is more easily digested than cows' milk. It is a simple matter to separate some of the fat from the whole milk. It can be left to rise to the surface and skimmed off as in cream, and it can be partially melted and resolidified, as in clotted cream. What the cheesemaker must do is to persuade the fat globules to become incorporated in the coagulating protein. There will always be some fat loss. Buttermaking leaves some fat in the buttermilk, cream leaves fat in the skim milk and cheese leaves some fat in the whey. Efficient handling of the curd will keep this fat loss to a minimum.

THE CARBOHYDRATES in the milk, mostly lactose or milk sugar, comprise 4-5% of the whole milk. About half this sugar will be converted by bacteria into lactic acid. The rest remains in the whey.

THE MINERALS, particularly calcium, are largely extracted from the milk as an essential part of the coagulation process and, together with some of the vitamins, they are included in the curd.

CHEESE is the result of the necessity to find a means of protecting the fresh milk from spoilage, and at the same time reducing its bulk. Nowadays this is done by a variety of means; sterilisation and bottling, condensing and adding sugar, drying, canning, and freezing; but long before the technology for these methods was available, making milk into cheese was the only way of preserving it.

To separate the solid part of the milk from the water, the cheesemaker utilises the natural coagulating properties of the protein, and by technique retains as much as possible of the other milk solids and fat.

Milk which has been left to go sour due to random bacterial action will coagulate and eventually separate, but this is not a wise way to make cheese. The bacteria responsible for the acid development in the curd should be those specially chosen for cheesemaking. Unselected bacteria can have undesirable effects. Some bacteria produce gases which cause 'blown' cheeses, cheeses with bulging or split rinds and centres full of round holes which are often shiny or slimy on the insides. Others produce unpleasant flavours or smells, turn the cheese an unacceptable colour or texture, and even in certain cases make it dangerous to eat.

Selected cheesemaking bacteria are added to the fresh milk at the beginning of the process, and they are encouraged to multiply and convert lactose to lactic acid.

By adding a quantity of active multiplying bacteria to the fresh warm milk, the cheesemaker hopes to ensure that these chosen bacteria take precedence over any random contamination.

STARTER is the name given to a culture of bacteria selected and prepared for cheesemaking. The most common available starters are a mixture of Streptococcus lactis and Streptococcus cremoris. Sometimes other streptococci and lactobacilli are added for flavour. Large scale, regular cheesemakers often use a series of mixed cultures. This is because bacteria are sensitive to one another and to other micro-organisms. The daily introduction of large quantities of the same organism into the equipment and premises increases the chances of those organisms becoming altered or infected and therefore less effective or even non-effective. It is unlikely that the home cheesemaker will encounter this problem, provided that good quality, freshly prepared starter is used at each cheesemaking.

After the starter has been added to the milk, the coagulation is assisted by the addition of an enzyme preparation.

STANDARD CHEESE RENNET is prepared from the enzyme rennin found in the stomachs of young calves. Junket rennet is of the same enzyme, but it is not of sufficient strength for cheesemaking. Vegetarian rennet is available from suppliers and is prepared from a similar enzyme produced by certain micro-organisms. There are a number of plants, the juices of which are reputed to have the necessary coagulating properties, but these are not readily available from normal sources.

When the curd is firm, it is broken or cut to release the whey. At this stage the curd is sometimes further hardened by gently heating or 'scalding' the mass of curds in the whey.

SALT. Most cheese contains salt. This improves the flavour and also assists in the separation of whey from the curd. The salt is always added in the latter stages of the process. Organisms cannot reproduce freely in salty conditions, and if the salt were added at the beginning the bacteria in the starter and therefore the acidity of the product would not develop at a suitable rate. Salt can be mixed with the curds before filling into molds, it can be rubbed or sprinkled over the surface of the cheese and/or the cheese can be immersed in a strong salt solution.

VEGETABLE DYE. Some cheese is artificially coloured to give a yellow or even an orange/red cheese. This is done by adding Annato — which is a vegetable dye prepared for the food industry. Annato for cheese colouring is in an alkaline solution, and it is important to add it to the milk before rennetting and before the acidity of the milk increases. Too acid conditions will bleach out the colour before it has become fixed in the curd.

CHAPTER TWO
PRACTICE

SUITABLE AND UNSUITABLE MILK. The quality of the cheese depends primarily on the quality of the milk. No cheesemaker, however skilled, can make good cheese out of tainted, spoiled or substandard milk.

Taints and off flavours which can be detected by smell and by taste may be caused by disease in the animal, by the animals' feeding, or by the handling of the milk after it leaves the udder. Cows that have been too long in milk, incomplete cleansing after calving, malnutrition or exhaustion, are all possible causes of bitter or salty milk. The overfeeding of turnips, kale, fish meal and other strong flavoured foods, and the accidental grazing of weeds such as garlic, camomile, bracken and hemlock will probably cause off flavours in the milk before the animal suffers any ill effect. But by far the most common cause of taint is the storing of the milk in close proximity to a strong smelling substance. Do not keep milk in a refrigerator at the same time as flavoured ice cream, onions, garlic, etc., and do not leave the milk container near the dung heap. It is also worth remembering that some plastic has a faintly perfumed smell which can easily be imparted to the milk when warm.

Spoiled milk which is suffering from bacterial contamination can again be the result of an unhealthy beast. If the milk is ropey or stringy to look at, or contains clots at milking, then the animal probably has mastitis, and milk from a beast who is in any way unwell is unlikely to be suitable for cheese. Milk which becomes contaminated after leaving the udder is certainly not suitable. Milking equipment, parlours, and all utensils must be scrupulously clean, and milk which is to be kept before use must be efficiently cooled and kept at a temperature of not more than 5°C, 41°F, until used. Always use a tightly covered vessel for transport and storage.

Substandard milk can be either deficient in content or contain undesirable substances. The butterfat and solids content of milk for cheesemaking should be average to high in

order to ensure a reasonable yield of finished cheese. Low
butterfat cheese will be hard and dry unless it is a cheese
specifically designed for skimmed milk. Very high butterfat
milk can be partially skimmed by hand before use to avoid
wasteful loss of fat to the whey.

Milk from a too recently calved cow can contain blood,
or traces of colostrum, which will spoil both the quality and
the look of the cheese, and any trace of antibiotics in the milk
will inhibit the development of the starter bacteria.

The most suitable milk for cheesemaking comes fresh
from a happy healthy cow milked under clean conditions,
with proper attention paid to the handling of the milk after it
leaves the udder.

Having obtained a supply of suitable milk, you must
decide whether to use it 'raw' or 'heat treated'. The majority
of commercially produced cheese in England is made from
pasteurised milk. This is thought necessary because the milk
comes from mixed sources and is bulked up and stored before
use. If you are happy that your milk is reliable and well
handled, then use it raw. Many people believe that the best
cheese is made with milk straight from the udder, either the
morning or the evening milking, and that having neither
cooled nor heat-treated the milk before use improves the
flavour and ripening quality of the cheese. If it is necessary to
mix the milks from more than one milking and the earlier milk
has been properly cooled, then it is perfectly all right to put
the milkings together and adjust the temperature of the
whole.

Heat treatment or pasteurisation is not easy to achieve in
the home. It is not recommended to treat any large quantity of
milk in a bucket on the stove. It takes too long to reach the
desired temperature of 154°F, 68°C, and the structure of the
milk begins to change. It is also impossible to cool the milk
quickly enough to be certain that no regrowth takes place
during the time that the milk is merely warm and therefore
most acceptable to micro-organisms.

If there is any doubt about the source of the raw milk or
its handling, and it is essential to pasteurise, then it is best to
invest in a home pasteuriser and to use it exactly according to

the instructions supplied. Pasteurisation will not make spoiled, tainted, or substandard milk good. All it will do is to make milk which might contain 'pathogenic' or health hazard bacteria into a substance temporarily safe for human consumpton.

Goats' milk and ewes' milk can be deep frozen and collected until there is enough for cheesemaking. It is not generally recommended to freeze cows' milk, but milk with ice in it, such as sometimes happens in a hard winter, makes perfectly good cheese, provided the temperature can be raised quickly to that required for the addition of starter.

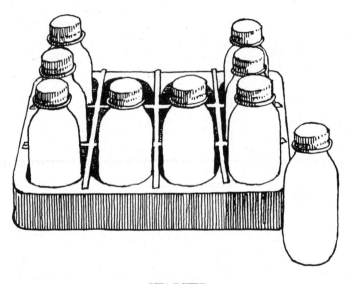

STARTER

STARTERS. Suitable cheese starter can be purchased from suppliers either freeze dried, as a powder, or in a liquid milk base. People making 100% goats' milk cheese are advised to use the dried starter, as the liquid culture is usually a cows' milk preparation.

Powdered starters should be prepared according to the manufacturer's instructions, and with careful management, both types of starter can be used to make a number of cheeses.

A very small amount of the original bacterial preparation added to more milk will multiply and produce more starter. This is called 'sub-culturing' and 'cultivation'. The original starter prepared from the commercial culture is known as the 'mother culture', and it is this mother culture which should be divided for future use. If the instructions recommend that the powder or the bottle or milk based starter should be added to, say, two litres of milk and kept in a warm place for twenty-four hours, then after keeping the two litres for twelve hours you can transfer some of the semi-mature mother culture to a number of sterile containers to be stored in a deep freeze. The contents of each one of these containers can be added to a further quantity of milk and matured for twenty-four hours before using to start cheese at a later date. Deep frozen cultures should remain active for at least six months. Use only the mother culture for storing. Sub-cultured starter has been exposed to the risk of contamination by unwanted micro-organisms, and the bacteria themselves are subject to a condition known as 'phage attack' which renders them inactive. There are micro-organisms everywhere — they are so minute that they are carried in the air. Not only bacteria, but also the spores or seeds of moulds and yeasts, which thrive in similar environments. Working beside a heat source reduces the risk of these airbourne organisms getting into your starter culture. Hot air rises, carrying the microbes with it. Work surfaces must be thoroughly cleaned, and all the vessels and utensils sterilised before use.

Some cheesemakers store their frozen cultures in plastic pots, such as those used for yoghurt and cream. Remember that plastic gets roughened with cleaning and can then contain grease traps. Check also that the lids fit properly. The ideal containers are small bottles with screw caps suitable for freezing. Mother culture can be matured in the saucepan in which the milk was boiled, but a plastic container, such as an ice cream container, is better. Cover the container with a clean cloth during the maturing period to protect the outside from dust and insect soiling. The quantities of mother culture to be stored will depend on the amount of starter needed at any one cheesemaking. One tablespoonful of active mother culture will make up to a pint of good starter. The amount of starter varies from cheese to cheese, but a pint of starter is sufficient for about ten gallons of milk. Having taken out some of the semi-mature mother culture for freezing, the rest can be matured for a further twelve hours and then used to start cheese.

Sometimes the matured starter will be lumpy and have solidified cream on the surface. Discard the creamy surface; it will float on the milk and cause yellow patches in the curd. Stir the starter thoroughly with a clean spoon and add it to the milk through a sieve or strainer. Lumps of starter do not mix in the milk and will appear as discolourations in the finished cheese. Never use old starter. It should be made up fresh for each batch of cheese. If you make too much starter, use it to make acid curd cheese. A little fresh milk can be used to increase the quantity, and the addition of whey gives an interesting texture. As a guide, use equal quantities of starter, milk, and whey mixed when warm, left overnight and then strained through a coarse cloth.

RENNET is added to the milk after the bacteriological starter, and in certain cases after a ripening period has elapsed. Dilute the rennet in 4 to 6 times the quantity of cold boiled water unless otherwise instructed in the recipe. Stir in thoroughly with a spoon long enough to reach to the bottom of the vessel containing the milk.

Concentrated rennet must be stored in a refrigerator. It has a long shelf life, but tends to lose strength gradually over the months. Even freshly purchased rennet varies slightly from bottle to bottle. The quantities given in the recipes are for 'standard cheese rennet'. If the coagulation period recommended does not result in a firm enough curd then increase the amount of rennet next time you make cheese, up to a further 0.5 ml per gallon of milk. If this is still insufficient, then change your rennet. You cannot add extra rennet once coagulation has begun. A weak curd can be left a little longer to see if it improves. If not, then carry on anyway. You will have a less than perfect cheese, but it will still be cheese, and used young should not be too dry. After the rennet has been added and stirred well in, it is essential to keep the top inch or so of the milk moving to prevent the fat from rising to the surface and subsequently being lost to the whey. This process is called 'top stirring'. Commercially this is done mechanically, but the best way to do this in the home is to trail the fingers, up to the first joint, in the milk and make 'waves'. When the waves take a long time to disappear, the milk is on the point of coagulating and top stirring must stop immediately or the curd will be broken too soon.

CURDS AND WHEY. When milk is coagulated by rising acidity and the addition of rennet, the whole of the milk coagulates, giving a curd with the consistency of junket or cold, thin custard. It is then necessary to break up this curd and release the whey. This is done either by ladling out the uncut curd in thin slices and allowing the whey to run from it, or by cutting the curd with knives, allowing it to sink and then draining off the surface liquid. It is important not to leave the coagulation process too long or the whey will begin to separate before cutting or ladling, and the draining will be uneven. Too short a coagulation time will give a curd so soft that it will break into crumbs and solids and fat will be lost to the whey. The right degree of coagulation can be judged by the 'clean break' method. This requires putting a finger into the curd and curling it up towards you. If the curd breaks with a clean split it is ready to cut. If it results in a milky pool, leave it longer to coagulate.

Whey escapes from the cut surface of the curd. Ladled curd should be ladled in thin slices as long as the ladle allows and laid in the cloth or mold carefully so as not to distort the area of cut surface. Folded slices and lumps of curd have too little drainage surface. Broken curd has too much.

Cut curd should be cut as nearly as possible into cubes of uniform size. A clean cut cube has six surfaces to drain. A bruised or crushed mass has very many more. The larger the number of irregular drainage surfaces, the more rapid and uneven the drainage, and the greater the loss of fat and solids to the whey.

It is possible with care and patience and very gentle handling to cut a bulk of curd with a household knife if curd knives are not available. The knife must be long enough to reach the bottom of the vessel containing the curd. It must be fine and sharp with a rounded end, not pointed. The curd is cut through to the bottom of the vessel in lines in both directions. One hand is then slid carefully down the side of the vessel and the pillars of curd are turned on their side up the forearm. Each strip of curd is then cut into cubes down its length and returned to the whey. Cutting and turning continues until all the cubes are of the size required for the cheese being made. There is always a lot of damaged curd when cut with a knife.

Special curd knives come in pairs. A vertical knife which has a series of blades set from top to bottom of a frame and a horizontal knife with blades set from side to side.

The knives should be held about once inch above and level with the surface of the curd. The end furthest from the handle is then allowed to slide into the curd as close to the side of the vessel as possible. The handle is raised gently until the base of the knife reaches the bottom of the vessel. Draw the knife carefully and firmly across the vessel and withdraw with a scooping movement, allowing the curd to fall through the blades. Do not knock the curd off. This will damage the curd, the knife, and the edge of the vessel. Occasionally a piece of curd will remain which is too large. This can be lifted on to the back of the hand and chopped with the vertical knife. People working in small circular vessels such as stew pans should lower the knife in the same manner and then cut in a spiral motion withdrawing at the centre. Large circular vessels of curd are cut in series from the centre to the sides along the radius, or across in the same manner as oval, oblong or square vessels.

It will take a considerable length of time for the whey to drain from the curd. This can be assisted by gently raising the temperature or scalding. During the early stages of drainage and during scalding, it is important to keep the cubes of curd

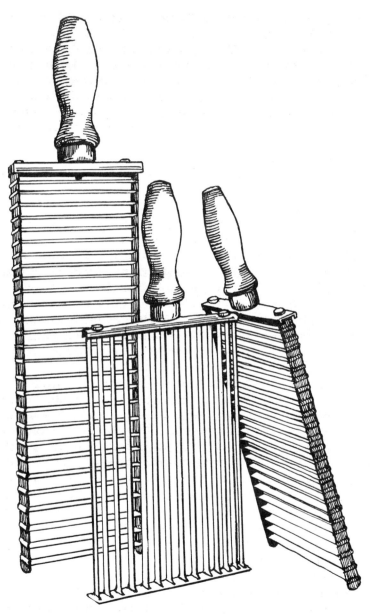

CURD KNIVES

moving, otherwise they will stick together in lumps and drainage faces will become sealed and drainage will become slow and uneven. In large quantities of curd, the stirring is done either mechanically or with a wooden rake, but in small quantities of curd, there is no better tool than the hand. If the hand is placed in the curd right to the bottom of the vessel, the cubes can be kept moving by gentle scooping movements and at the same time prevented from sticking to the bottom of the vessel during heating.

After sufficient initial drainage has taken place and scalding has been completed, the curd is allowed to sink to the bottom of the vessel and consolidate in the whey. This is called 'pitching'.

During the drainage and scalding, the activity of the bacteria will have continued to raise the acidity of the whey. Acidity control plays a very important part in the production of cheese where it is essential to produce an identical product at every cheesemaking, but in home cheesemaking it is probably sufficient to be sure that the acidity continues to rise steadily to the required level. For this the curd must be kept warm, but not hot, at all times right up to milling and molding, or in the case of soft cheese, to removal from the mold or cloth.

The 'drawing of the whey' or removal of the whey from around the consolidated curd follows the pitching. If the vessel has a drain or tap, this is a fairly simple matter, but a curd strainer or small sieve must be held over the drain to prevent the escape of small curd particles not adherring to the main mass. Where no tap is fitted, the whey is baled out of the vessel with a jug or bowl and poured into the whey bucket through a sieve. Rescued particles of curd should be returned to the mass before they have time to get cold. Pushing up the curd mass to one end of the vessel helps to make whey drawing easier and the vessel can be tilted slightly. Do not tilt too far or the curd mass will slide. The last drops of whey can be soaked up with a cheese cloth, which after wringing out can be used to keep the curd blocks warm.

The method of dividing the blocks of curd in the vessel or cloth varies from cheese to cheese, but all types of cheese require that the curd is kept warm until ready for molding. Small amounts of curd lose heat faster than large ones. A towel or similar cloth wrapped around and over the vessel helps to keep the warmth in.

When the curd is ready for molding, it will be broken into smaller pieces or 'milled'. Some semi-soft cheeses are crumbled before molding, but most hard and semi-hard cheeses are milled to a specific size. Curd mills are available for commercial large scale production, either 'chip mills' which chop the curd into cubes, or 'peg mills' which tear it into lumps. Hand milling is similar to the action of a peg mill. A piece of curd is taken in one hand and with the finger and thumb of the other hand tear off pieces of the required size.

Salting instructions are given with each individual recipe as are the actual molding and pressing requirements.

The first requirement is THE MILK CONTAINER or carrier, for collecting the milk from the dairy or milking parlour. Remember that milk weighs 10¼ lbs per gallon. It is better to have two smaller containers than one so heavy when filled that it is inconvenient to lift. It must have a neck wide enough to allow a hand through so that it can be properly cleaned, and be of odourless, sterilisable material. Ideally it should have a well fitting spillproof lid and strong handles which give a good grip.

If the milk is to be transported by vehicle, the container should be able to stand upright in transit. A conventional milk churn may be too tall.

ANOTHER CONTAINER about 2 litre capacity will be needed for collecting milk for starter production.

THE MAJOR VESSEL OR VAT. A bucket or pail is all right for soft cheese production. Ideally it should be stainless steel, but good quality odour free plastic will do. Soft cheese curd can be kept warm by standing the bucket in warm water, and as scalding is either not indicated, or there is to be only a slight temperature rise, this can be achieved by raising the temperature of the surrounding water. It the milk to be used has been cooled after leaving the udder, then the bucket will have to be metal so that it can be placed on the stove. Galvanised iron is not suitable, tin plate should be sound and rust free, and the bucket should be without a deep rim at the bottom, so that there is direct contact with the heat source.

For cheese in which the curd is to be cut as opposed to ladled out, a bucket is not really suitable; the ratio of depth to diameter makes good cutting difficult. A preserving pan or catering sized saucepan is much better. They are not too deep and have large flat bottoms. The ideal vessel is oblong or square. It is more efficient to cut in straight lines than along curves. If it is possible to have a drain or tap fitted to the vessel, this makes the drawing of the whey easier, but it is not essential. It is quite possible to bale the whey off. Of course every cheesemaker would like ideal equipment. A stainless steel water-jacketed vat with independent heating, complete with drain tap and curd strainer would probably be very expensive, and it would not necessarily improve the cheese.

The selected vessel must be of such size and weight that it can be lifted on and off the stove when full. It is not possible to make cheese, such as Cheddar, where the curd is to be stacked and turned, in a bucket. The base of the vessel must be large enough to allow the whey to drain away from the blocks of curd.

MINOR VESSELS

1. *A saucepan* for boiling milk for starter — with a close fitting lid if the starter is to mature in the same vessel. It is probably better to transfer the boiled milk to another container before adding the mother culture. Plastic boxes and basins with snap-on lids are excellent.

2. *Storage containers* for frozen mother culture. Ideally screw capped bottles. The wads must be removed from the caps before use and not replaced.

3. *Bowls or jugs* for dipping whey. A small straight sided plastic sandwich box is useful for drawing the last inch of whey from the vessel. The bowls for dipping the whey should be unbreakable. Plastic mixing bowls are good. These can also be used for catching the whey from 'bag cheese' or cheese hung in a cloth, and for standing filled molds in to catch the drainage. If the shape of the bowl is such that the mold can rest part way down, then the cheese can rest above the drained whey.

4. *A cup or small bowl* for diluted rennet. If an acid meter is to be used, then the same bowl will do.

5. *A selection of pots* and containers for cottage curd cream cheese and plastic boxes for storing molded curd cheese in the refrigerator.

6. *A spare bucket* containing weak hypochlorite solution is useful for dropping cloths and used equipment into during the actual cheesemaking.

Other vessels and containers may be needed from time to time. These can often be found amongst everyday household equipment, but they must be thoroughly clean and odour-free.

DRAINERS. Where a curd drainer is indicated, it is possible to use a colander or the top of a steamer, but a perforated stainless rack on supports is better when the curd blocks are to be laid out. Catering steamer tops will be useful, particularly for those cheesemakers using the steamer bottom as their major vessel, and some catering saucepans come with suspended drainers to fit. It is possible to drain bags of curd in plastic boxes with holes drilled in them, or even in large plastic flower pots.

Molded soft curd cheese and molded semi-hard cheese can be drained on the draining board beside the sink provided they can be left undisturbed or on a spare draining board which can be moved out of the way as soon as the curd is firm enough. A large roasting pan with a ridged base can be utilised. This will need frequent emptying which presents complications as moving often causes the curd to spill from the mold. It is better to soak up the whey from the pan with cloths.

A flour sieve makes a good curd strainer provided the curd can be cleaned from the mesh. Use plastic or stainless rather than tin plate.

THERMOMETERS. A thermometer is essential; the 'dairy maid's elbow' is not accurate enough. Floating dairy thermometers are the best, but if this is not available, an ordinary thermometer will do; not a clinical thermometer or a jam boiling thermometer, and a ten inch is better than a six inch. If the thermometer is pushed through a hole bored in a large cork, it should float, which will prevent broken glass, alcohol or mercury getting into the cheese should the thermometer be accidently dropped. Either °F or °C will do. A conversion table is included at the back of this book.

A wall thermometer is useful in the cheese store. These are available, either separately or combined with humidity gauges, from garden supply stores. A wall thermometer can be used in the kitchen or cheesemaking room. But room temperature can be read with the milk thermometer.

ACID METERS. The acid development in the curd is important to the quality of the cheese, but being able to measure the degree of acidity at each stage is not essential. Good cheese was being made before acid meters were invented. Development was measured by timing, texture, and smell, together with the strange concept of the 'Hot Iron Test'. The hot iron test required the touching of a piece of curd to a hot iron and measuring the length of cheese thread which could be pulled before it broke. No temperature other than hot was given for the iron, but it was assumed that the thread length was a measure of acid development. It is far more reasonable to assume that it was merely a rule of thumb for texture and would be infinitely variable depending on the heat of the iron, the temperature of the room and the speed of the 'pull'.

The only reliable way of measuring the acidity of the milk or whey is by using an acid meter. This instrument is comprised of a container of alkaline solution — N/9 Sodium Hydroxide — to which is attached a 'burette' or graduated column marked from 1 to 10 with a delivery tube at the bottom. With this comes a bottle of 'indicator' — a 1% solution of phenolpthalein, a dropper, a 10 ml pipette or measuring glass and a small bowl. Phenolpthalein indicator is colourless, but turns pink in alkaline solution. The principle behind the use of this apparatus is based on the amount of alkaline solution of a known strength needed to neutralise a known amount of acid solution of an unknown strength. 10 ml of milk or whey are placed in the bowl. Indicator is added and the sodium hydroxide solution is run into the bowl from the burette. The contents of the bowl must be stirred whilst adding the alkaline solution. When the whey or milk mixture

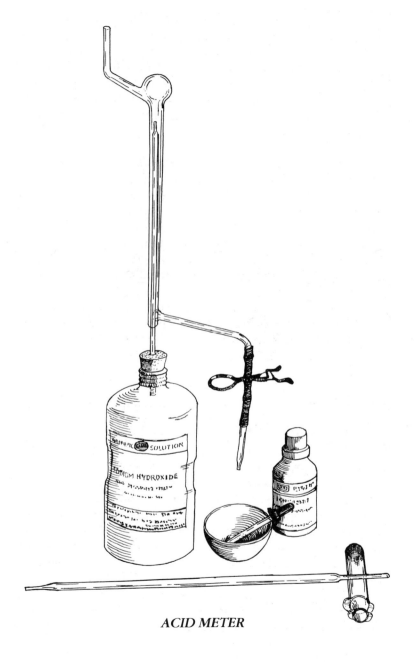

ACID METER

turns and stays slightly pink, the burette reading is taken. Most cheese recipes which include acidity readings quote the direct reading from the burette, i.e. 0.15% or an acidity of 1.5 will mean that the level of solution remaining in the burette will be halfway between the graduations marked one and two. Each $\frac{1}{10}$ ml of the alkaline solution neutralises 0.001 grammes of lactic acid, which in a 10 ml whey or milk sample is interpreted as 0.01% acidity.

BOARDS. It is advisable to have a number of boards of different sizes so that there is always a clean dry one ready for turning cheese onto. Small boards, just big enough to stand the mold on, are safer when turning delicate curd. Boards should be made of close textured, non-resinous, non-aromatic timber, and should not stain the cloths or curd. They should be sanded down, but not painted or varnished. Most d.i.y. shops and timber merchants can supply suitable offcuts.

MATS. Special reed cheese mats are available from suppliers, but it is possible to use straw or reed table mats provided they are colourfast and that the weave can be scrubbed free of curd particles.

CLOTHS. Three types of cheesecloths are recommended, cheese grey, cheesecloth and muslin. Cheese grey is a coarse texture cloth — for which can be substituted certain loose-weave cotton household textiles. Cheesecloth is available from dairy suppliers and also from most fabric shops. It is advisable to purchase the proper thing — old sheeting can be used, but it is neither as absorbent nor as moldable and tends to mark the skin of the cheese. Muslin is also available in most fabric shops. Cotton lawn will do as well. Do not use loose weave muslin, except for bandaging after pressing. During pressing fine muslin tends to become molded to the curd and the skin of the cheese is broken when the cloth is removed.

Cheesecloth should be used for the first day in press and thick muslin for the finishing days. Cheese grey or other coarse cloth is best for straining curd and for making 'bag' cheeses. Curd fills the weave of finer fabrics and draining is slowed down. This means that the curd will have to be scraped down more often, which can spoil the texture. Keep the size of press cloths as small as will just line the mold and fold over the top of the curd. Excess fabric marks the surface of the cheese. One large piece of cloth is useful for draining off whey. It must be large enough to line the whey bucket and be held firmly all the way round. If it is intended to drain the whey directly down the sink, then the cloth must totally line the sink and be weighted or anchored all the way round. It is easy to lose both curds and whey down the drain by using too small a cloth. The large cloths are also useful for covering cheese in the press and during the drying stage.

A quantity of rags which can be discarded after use are helpful when cleaning mould from maturing cheese. It is better to throw the wiping cloth away than to try to get it clean enough for re-use. In a cheese store which is not totally insect proof, the maturing cheeses must be protected from flyblow and other insect damage by covering with close weave net or ideally mosquito netting. Useful cheese 'tents' can be made like small wigwams. Metal coat hangers can be bent to make the framework, or even better, a tower saucepan rack will make a safe tent for several cheeses.

LADLES, SPOONS, KNIVES, ETC. A stainless steel ladle is best. It should have a fine unfolded edge to the bowl, which should be fairly shallow and small enough to lower into the soft cheese molds so that the slices of curd can be laid in and not poured from above. Make sure the handle is at the right angle for scooping curd from the major vessel, i.e. at a right angle to the plane of the rim of the bowl.

Ordinary household tablespoons are fine for measuring starter — each spoonful can be reckoned as 15 ml — but a wooden spoon, long enough to reach the bottom of the vessel will be necessary for stirring the milk after adding the starter and after renneting. Teaspoons are misleading. Only those which are supplied with medicines are a guaranteed 5 ml. Some household teaspoons actually hold as little as 3.5 ml. A 5 ml teaspoon is a great help for measuring rennet. In recipes

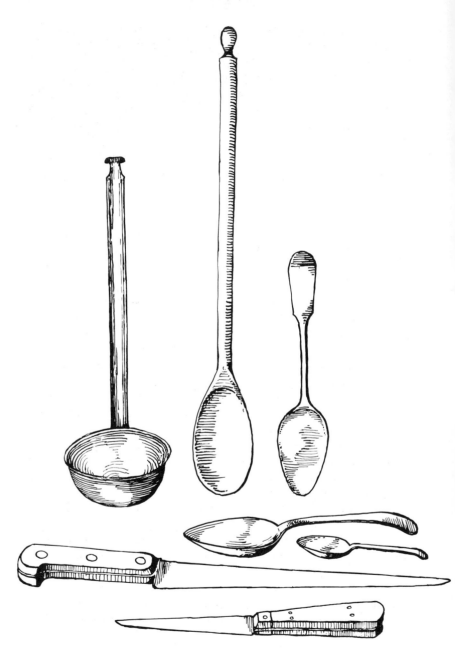

LADLE, SPOONS AND KNIVES

26

where the pitched curd is cut into blocks, in the absence of a curd knife it is best to use a long sharp knife. A carving knife will do, particularly if it has a fine slender blade. If the size of vat makes a long knife awkward to handle, use a good kitchen knife of similar style but smaller size. Some cheesemakers transfer curd with a cream skimmer or draining spoon. This is not really good cheesemaking practice, but in the absence of a ladle, it should work. Ideally the whey should enter the mold with the curd. The predraining caused by using a skimmer or spoon with holes in it is likely to produce a much drier textured cheese.

MOLDS. *For soft cheese.* There is a traditional size and shape for most of the better known soft cheeses. Molds are available from suppliers, both in plastic and in metal, but there is considerable variation in both size and price from one manufacturer to another.

Soft cheeses can be made in improvised molds. Carefully chosen and cleaned cans with tops and bottoms removed are good. Select cans which are undamaged and rust and smell free. Clean them thoroughly before use and discard them as soon as they show signs of rusting. Individual portions can be made in pastry cutters or serviette rings.

A *typical coulommier* mold is made in two parts. A bottom ring approximately 5" x 3½" and a top ring approximately 5" x 2¼". The two rings fit together. The whole mold is filled with curd and the top ring is removed when the curd has settled sufficiently. This makes the frequent turning of this delicate cheese less risky and the finished cheese almost fills the bottom ring.

A *Pont L'Eveque* mold is oblong, approximately 5¾" x 3¾" and 2" deep.

A *Colwick mold* is like a small round cake tin with sides and bottom perforated. Colwick can be made in a Camembert mold, or any other small round former.

A *Camembert mold* is 5" diameter, 5" deep, round, and drilled all over with small holes and has no base plate. Camembert can be made in a Coulommier mold or a cleaned can.

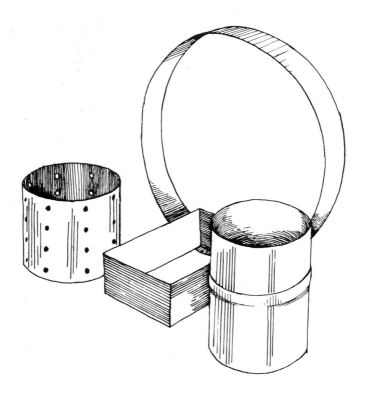

MOLDS

Cream and cottage cheeses used to be molded in sets of small round molds lined with greaseproof paper, but nowadays plastic pots are more usual. These cheeses look nice if wrapped in vine leaves or presented in rush baskets. Many different sorts of baskets and tubs are available, very often as plantpots holders. Make sure they are colourfast and odour-free and sterilise them before use.

For hard and semi hard cheese. Molds for unpressed or lightly pressed cheese can be purchased from suppliers both in plastic and in metal. The size of mold depends on the size of cheese to be made. A circular mold 6" diameter with a depth of 7½" will hold about 4 lb of curd. Although there is no necessity to make round cheeses, most available molds are this shape, and it is probably the most easy to handle. Make sure the mold is smooth on the inside with no projections which can catch on the cloth or tear the skin of the cheese when turning. They should have firm smooth rims, top and bottom, as it is sometimes necessary to knock the mold on the table to release the cheese. Use only molds made of material that will not taint your cheese and preferably of a rust proof nature.

Weights for light pressing can be improvised, providing the mold is supplied with a firm flat 'follower' or fitted disc on which to apply the pressure. This can be either wood, plastic or metal. It is advisable to use a mold fitted with a base plate of perforated plastic or metal.

Molds for pressed cheeses must be strong enough to take the pressure to be applied and must have firm smooth sides and rims which will not buckle. They should have fitted base plates and must be supplied with followers. A smooth metal or plastic plate gives a better finish at the final pressing. Make sure that the finishing plate is a good fit otherwise the cheese will need trimming when removed from the press. Small irregularities in the surface of the cheese usually disappear during storage. The mold must be perforated to allow the whey to escape, and the holes should not be so large that the cheese is pushed through them, nor so small that they become blocked by cloth and curd. Perforations reaching at least half way up the mold are better that just a few at the bottom.

PRESSES. Most commercial cheesemakers now use what is known as a 'gang press'. This is a horizontal row of tapered molds with followers which just fit into one another. Hydraulic pressure is applied and transferred from one mold to the next. Before these presses were available the 'lever arm press' was most common. Here pressure was applied vertically to the top of the mold and follower by a fixed plate which screwed down into the mold. Pressing was assisted by levers and weights. Many of these presses are now in museums but, when in working order, they are capable of adaptation to the home cheesemaker's requirements, and can sometimes be found at farm sales and auctions. If a number of small cheeses are to be made, the overall pressure of the fixed plate will have to be spread over the small molds by adding extra followers as the cheese goes down into the mold so that

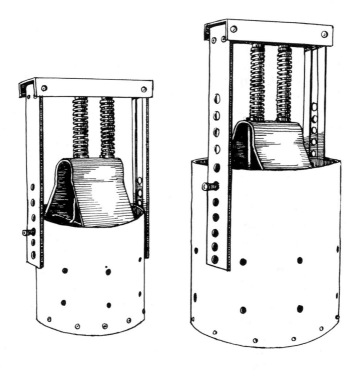

MOLDS AND PRESSES

the follower is always above the rim of the mold and in contact with the press plate. Individual presses and molds, of which there are at least three different models on the market, are probably best for the small scale home cheesemaker. Again there is wide variety in design and price.

There is considerable confusion over the amount of pressure which should be applied to each variety of cheese. Instructions on pressing, when they appear at all, are often in such vague terms as 'screw pressure only' — no indication is given as to how much pressure the screw applies or even whether it has been screwed down by hand or with the aid of a lever. Even more precise instructions such as '6 cwt pressure' are meaningless unless the size of the cheese is known. In texts where the pressing weight is given together with a cheese size, it is possible to work out the amount of pressure in terms of lbs per square inch, i.e. p.s.i., but unfortunately these rarely agree one with the other and in some cases would appear to be nonsense.

The purpose of pressing cheese at all is primarily to consolidate the curd and mold it to a pleasing shape. It does at the same time expel an amount of whey, but where the curd has been properly worked before milling and molding, this will not be great.

The legal requirements for marketing cheese lays down a maximum water content for a number of named varieties. It therefore follows that the correct amount of pressure for these varieties of cheese is that which will consolidate and mold the curd and expell any moisture in excess of the legal limit. The actual amount of pressure measured in p.s.i. which will achieve this is surprisingly small. It has been shown that over a 6" diameter Cheddar cheese, spring pressure of 56 lb (which on calculation gives 2 p.s.i.) is sufficient to give cheese of a good texture with a water content of less than 38%. No actual pressures are given in this book beyond such terms as light, medium, and maximum. The type of press used will determine how this can best be judged. Spring controlled presses are at maximum pressure when the springs are fully depressed. To maintain maximum pressure over the pressing period, it will be necessary to readjust the press frequently or to add followers to take up the space in the mold as the cheese shrinks.

OTHER EQUIPMENT

Spring clothes pegs are perfect for holding cloths round buckets or sinks.

One inch strips cut from nylon stockings are far better than string for tying up bags of curd. They can be looped round the ends of cloth instead of tied and are much easier to remove when wet.

Metal skewers or knitting needles are good for 'needling' blue cheeses.

Pieces of greaseproof paper in small squares, appropriately marked in pencil can be greased onto the surface of cheeses for identification during storage. Biro and ink fade and run. Use a blunt pencil on the uppermost side of the label only, and it will still be readable after the mould has been wiped off the surface many times. Date the cheese, and mark with the letter of the variety, i.e. C for Cheddar, Ca for Caerphilly, Le for Leicester, etc. It is also advisable to keep a diary or 'cheesebook'. Mark in this any variations from the recipe or any problems encountered. This will help to explain faults, control usage dates and also to repeat an especially good cheese.

CARE AND CLEANING OF EQUIPMENT

Everything used in cheesemaking should be thoroughly clean and preferably sterilised. This means free of all micro-organisms. It is not possible to achieve total sterility in the home, but by taking careful precautions, it is possible to reduce contamination to an acceptable level. All trace of previous usage must be removed. Wash first in cold water to remove the milk. Hot water coagulates the milk protein and makes the particles difficult to remove.

Utensils should then be washed, scrubbed and scoured with hot water and non-perfumed detergent. Liquid detergent is better than powder, as powder particles can remain undissolved in irregularities on the surface of the equipment. Scouring pads can be used on metal vessels and

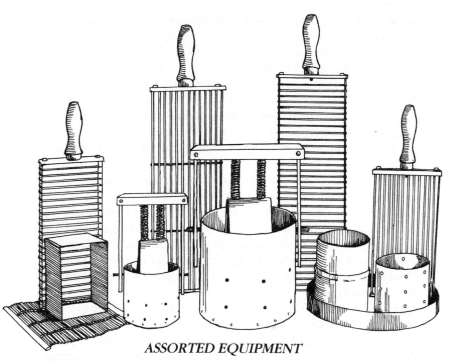

ASSORTED EQUIPMENT

molds, but not on plastic where they will roughen the surface. If steel wool is used, be careful that no small pieces of wire are trapped. These can go rusty and also be transferred to the curd. Pay special attention to debris and grease traps such as hollow handles, rims, seams, screw or rivet heads and manufacturing irregularities. Follow this thorough washing with repeated rinsing to remove all traces of cleaning agents. Large items, such as milk carriers and major vessels can be washed in the bath; sinks are rarely large enough to accommodate the vessel so that it is cleaned equally well outside as in. Protect the surface of the bath with cloths or plastic sheeting.

Steam treatment, as in a pressure cooker, or lengthy boiling (a 'rolling' boil for at least 30 minutes) can follow, but this is only practical for the smaller items. By far the easiest method of sterilisation is to soak everything in a solution of sodium hypochlorite. Most household bleaches are hypochlorite solutions. The label must be read carefully to make sure that nothing has been added such as 'surfactants' or 'deodorisers'. There will be variations in the strength and therefore the sterilising power from brand to brand. The manufacturer's recommended strength for 'whites' in the washing will certainly be more than adequate for the sterilisation of equipment. Commercial dairy cleaners which are hypochlorite solutions usually carry instructions on recommended strengths for specific uses. The hypochlorite should not be used too strong. If it smells like a public swimming pool, it is unnecessarily powerful.

After soaking, rinse everything lightly and leave to drain. Do not wipe dry — even a clean tea towel is capable of spreading contaminants such as mould spores. If the utensils are not of a rust proof nature they can be dried quickly in a warm oven to prevent rusting. Mains water users can do their final rinsing under the cold tap. Others may be well advised to use boiled water.

Cloths can be put through the washing machine after the first cold rinse; check carefully for curd caught in the weave, and then use the washing programme for whites. It is not advisable to wash them with other items as cheesecloth tends to fluff in the washing. Empty the fibre trap in the machine and make sure the rinsing is very thorough. If washing by hand, be certain that all suds and debris have been removed. Ideally cloths should then be boiled or soaked in hypochlorite, rinsed again, and dried in the sunlight. Fresh air and sunlight remove every last trace of chlorine and leave cloths softer, but they should be protected from birds, flies and other soiling creatures.

Curd knives will need careful scrubbing with a long bristled brush, especially round the handle and in the area where the blades join the frame. They must then be washed and sterilised as other utensils.

Mats and boards can be scrubbed with the same brush. A longer soaking time should be given to boards, both in the first cold wash and also in the hypochlorite solution. These also will benefit from drying in fresh air and sunlight. Try not to use frayed or damaged mats or split boards. It is not easy to remove small curd particles from cracks in the wood or split mat fibres.

Bottles for starter culture need special care. If caps contain wads, they must be removed, discarded and not replaced. Paper and fibre wads are a constant source of contamination. Rinse bottles and caps in cold water, brush thoroughly with a bottle brush, hot water and detergent inside and out, particularly round the thread of the cap and bottleneck. Rinse thoroughly and sterilise. These can be put in a pressure cooker, or they can be filled to the top with hypochlorite solution and then immersed together with their caps, but not with their caps on, in a container filled with a similar solution. After soaking, bottles and caps must be emptied and rinsed with boiled water. When completely drained, the caps are put back on the bottles and the outsides rinsed again. Rinse thoroughly; even a drop of hypochlorite remaining can spoil the activity of the starter.

If the bottles are not to be re-used immediately, the caps are screwed down tightly for storage. The outsides of the bottles must be re-sterilised before use, and if a long time has elapsed since cleaning the whole process should be repeated.

CHAPTER FOUR
PREMISES

ANYBODY setting out to make cheese for sale will need their premises inspected and approved by the local authority (see chapter 5), but the well equipped kitchen contains all the basic requirements for home cheesemaking. The premises should have a sink with running water, a stove or cooker, work tops, and preferably floor space enough for milk containers and whey buckets. In houses with small kitchenettes or galleys, it may be possible to use the utility room or laundry, and the wash houses, still rooms, and sculleries of older properties can make excellent cheese rooms.

It is possible to work without a stove or cooker, but only if considerable quantities of hot water are available, and the sink is large enough to hold the vessel full of curd and surround it with hot water. Even then it is rarely wholly satisfactory.

It is obviously best to make cheese in a warm room free of draughts; this prevents the problem of slow working chilled curd. However, during the history of cheesemaking it must have been made successfully under very different conditions, and even recently, 8 lbs of good Cheddar were made in a tent in a field on a wet windy day! (See Author's Notes).

A solid fuel or oilfired stove is excellent. It keeps the room warm, and at the same time provides the heat source for adjusting milk and curd temperature. Electric or gas cookers can do both these jobs if the oven is left on during the process. The ideal room temperature is 75°F, 24°C.

The working area should be made as clean as possible before starting. Work surfaces should be easy to clean. Old unvarnished wood soaks up spilt milk and whey and will harbour unwanted bacteria. Slate and marble may be cleanable, but they will absorb heat from anything placed upon them and would have to be covered with boards or cloths to prevent this. Plastic surfaces or well varnished wood are the most suitable.

All surfaces should be wiped down, first with warm water and detergent and then with a cloth wrung out in hypochlorite solution. The sink should be cleaned, and domestic rubbish disposed of. All bread, fruit, beer, and wine should be put away, and cheese and yoghurt should never be made together. The yeasts from bread and brewing can ruin cheese, and the bacteria in yoghurt may be incompatible with those in the cheese starter.

All equipment should be clean and readily to hand and there must be a supply of fresh active starter. It is wise to close doors and windows to keep in warmth and keep out dust.

A clean apron or towel round the waist of the cheesemaker will protect the clothes from the cheese and the cheese from the clothes. Long hair should be tied back. Not only does hair contain dust, but a hair in the curd is almost impossible to remove. Short finger nails are least likely to harbour micro-organisms. Nails should be free of nail varnish as this is likely to 'lift' in the whey and be left in the curd.

Cheesemaking should be timed carefully. Molded soft cheese will have to drain undisturbed for up to 24 hours. If the domestic draining board is used, the kitchen cheesemaker will encounter difficulties in washing up and preparing the everyday meals. A second drainer is a great asset, and a moveable one can be carefully removed to another area once the initial drainage is over and the cheese can be moved without spilling out of the mold.

Scalded and pressed cheeses will 'take over' the cooker for several hours, and their making should be timed not to clash with normal meals.

Provision must be made for locating the cheese press and filled molds. Individual molds and presses can remain in the kitchen until ready to leave the press. They will have to sit in bowls or on drainage trays for up to four days, but these can be moved to any other suitable location. Keep them covered with clean cloths, and if the room is permanently heated, or the weather hot, keep the cloths damp. Large lever arm presses will have to be located in a place set aside for them. They are much too big for the average kitchen.

Before deciding to make cheese, proper provision must be made for maturing and storage. Soft cheeses can go straight from the drainer to a refrigerator, unless they are for ripening, in which case a flyproof, ventilated container, such as an old meat safe, which can be put in a suitable outhouse, is advisable. Do not try to mature Camembert or Brie in the house. It may do well, but the smell will permeate everything.

Hard and semi-pressed cheeses need a drying off period after leaving the mold. This can be done in the kitchen, again with the aid of cloths, provided it is not too warm; a temperature of 65°F, 18°C is reasonable. After drying off, the success or failure of the finished cheese will depend upon the conditions in the storage area. The ideal conditions for most cheeses are found in the cool damp cellars of older properties. Cool walk-in larders are nearly as good. Disused coal sheds, provided the smell of coal tar has gone, barns, outbuildings, and even the old privy are all possibles, and a block-built cupboard in a shaded, sheltered, place could be the answer. Wherever the store is located, it must be cool and moist, vermin and flyproof. The fly problem can be overcome by making cheese sized 'tents' out of netting and wire. The mesh of the netting must be small enough to exclude the small flies which can leave maggots just as unpleasant as those of larger flies. The cheese store must also be reasonably accessible for the daily turning of the cheese, and the cleaning and inspection thereafter. The cheesemaker who has none of these facilities can make a satisfactory cheese store out of a large refrigerator provided there is a suitable setting on the thermostat. The temperature should hold between 13°-15°C, 55°-60°F. Remove the door seal to allow air flow and a pan of water placed in the bottom during dry weather will help to maintain the humidity level.

Ideal conditions for storage are a temperature of 13°-15°C, 55°-60°F, and 85-95% humidity. Too high a temperature or insufficient humidity can cause shrunken skins, which spoil the shape and the look of the cheese, and sometimes the skins crack or split allowing moulds to enter. Too low a temperature slows maturing and can spoil the flavour, and too moist an atmosphere can give a slimy skin and permit bacterial growth. Some surface mould growth is inevitable and indeed desirable, but too much can be a nuisance. If it is possible to mature blue or mould-inoculated cheese separately, this is a good idea.

The shelves on which the cheeses are to stand should be slatted and of untreated timber. If it is necessary to use plastic faced material or metal, the cheeses must be stood on racks and mats to prevent 'sweating' on the surface in contact with the shelf.

Occasionally cheese mites appear in the store. The store should be constructed in such a manner that it can be thoroughly cleaned and fumigated to destroy mites and unwanted moulds.

CHAPTER FIVE
LEGISLATION

IF CHEESE is made for personal consumption, it may be called by whatever name the cheesemaker chooses to give it, and may be made to any standard and under any conditions of hygiene.

There are no regulations to protect individuals from the product of their own manufacture except, perhaps, practicality and common sense. However, those producers who wish to sell their excess production, or even a commodity containing their product, are required by law to comply with a variety of regulations.

Firstly those regulations relating specifically to cheese, followed by the wider scope of those regulations governing the premises in which cheese is made, the premises in which cheese is sold, the personal cleanliness and welfare of persons engaged in production or selling, and finally the labelling, packaging, and advertising of the product.

The various regulations run to many pages of official language, which may appear somewhat daunting to the would-be producer. However, on careful study, it becomes obvious that the requirements are no more than common sense, and precisely what the cheesemaker would demand were he or she a discerning customer rather than the producer.

It is not intended that this chapter should cover every legal facet of cheese manufacture and sale, rather that it should outline the basic legal requirements and inform cheesemakers intending to sell their products where to look for the proper advice. Copies of all the regulations quoted are available from H.M.S.O. and certain bookshops by ordering, or may be examined at many central libraries.

THE FOOD HYGIENE (GENERAL) REGULATIONS 1970 (S.I. No. 1172)

The manufacture or handling of any food for human consumption must be carried out in such a manner as to avoid contamination of that food which could lead, at the most, to death, and at the least, to the displeasure of the consumer.

As contamination of one sort or another, dirt, flies, vermin, bacteria, etc., can come from a variety of sources, the regulations cover all facets of food handling. The fact that cheese, particularly hard cheese, is virtually unknown as a source of illness, does not lessen the fact that as a food it must comply with the regulations.

The general requirements of the Food Hygiene Regulations are as follows:

The premises in which food is handled must be suitable for the purpose. They must be sanitary, drained by an appropriate system, and have adequate supplies of clean, hot and cold water. They must be properly ventilated, and well lit. The premises must contain toilet, washing, first-aid, and locker facilities for persons working there, and these facilities must not be part of, or immediately lead out of, the food handling areas. All reasonable precautions must be taken to exclude vermin and insects from the premises and the state of the structure and decoration must be such as to allow effective cleaning.

The equipment used in the handling or manufacture of the product must be suitable for the purpose and must be easily cleanable in facilities other than those provided for personal cleanliness.

The product and its ingredients must, at all times, be protected from contamination. The storage of refuse and waste products must be away from the premises, in suitable places where disposal can take place regularly.

Personal cleanliness of a high standard must be maintained. Notices reminding people to wash their hands must be displayed in the appropriate places. Protective clothing must be worn, and in some cases, this must include headgear. In the event of certain infectious diseases occurring, the appropriate authority must be informed.

Transportation and wrapping of the product must be carried out in the proper manner.

There are provisions in the regulations for the storage in catering establishments of certain perishable foods at either high or low temperatures. Cheese is excluded (para. 27/f), but it is doubtful whether certain curd cheeses are meant to be a part of the exclusion. Special advice should be sought by producers intending to sell soft cheese.

THE MILK AND DAIRIES (GENERAL) REGULATIONS 1959 (S.I. No. 277)

These regulations require that any premises used for the handling of milk or milk products must be registered with the appropriate Local Authority. The Local Authority may have additional requirements.

THE FOOD HYGIENE (MARKETS, STALLS AND DELIVERY VEHICLES) REGULATIONS 1966 (S.I. 791)

With the handling of food during manufacture carefully controlled, it is then necessary to regulate its handling during distribution and sale. These regulations are of relevance to the cheesemaker who intends to retail their product. The requirements are very similar to those relating to the handling of food in the 'General' regulations, except that the emphasis is placed on the construction, siting and cleanliness of stalls, markets and delivery vehicles rather than on 'premises'. The necessity for personal and equipment washing facilities, protection from contamination, personal cleanliness, wearing of protective clothing, notification of infectious diseases, care with carriage and wrapping, etc., are all included plus the additional requirement of the display on the stall, market, or vehicle of the name and address of the person trading.

Apart from the legislation that provides for the care in handling food both during manufacture and sale, there are other legal requirements of trading to be considered. The rules covering the labelling of food generally, are contained in the LABELLING OF FOOD REGULATIONS 1980 (S.I. 1849) and more specifically, cheese is covered in the CHEESE REGULATIONS 1970 S.I. No. 94). Basically the regulations call for clear, precise and prominent labelling of the product and specify requirements for any advertising. Such labelling must describe the cheese exactly, either by variety or composition (further details of these classifications are given later in the chapter) and no inference by word or picture must be made that the cheese is anything more or less than it is.

THE WEIGHTS AND MEASURES REGULATIONS 1963 (S.I. 1970) are also important. With subsequent amendments they relate to all kinds of sales by weight, volume, and size. In the case of cheese, there is an obligation to use certified scales and to fulfil whatever declared weight of product is offered for sale. See also Weights and Measures Act 1963 (Cheese) Order 1977, (S.I. No. 1335) and the Price Marking (Cheese) Order 1977 (S.I. No. 1344).

THE HEALTH AND SAFETY AT WORK ACT 1974 (S.I. No. 1439) lays down that various precautions must be taken to ensure that a worker's health and safety is not put at risk by foolish or negligent practices. This *does not exclude* self-employed cheesemakers from responsibility towards themselves and other people. Although cheesemaking may not appear to be a hazardous occupation, the weights to be lifted can be heavy and cause injury. Floors can be slippery and electrical equipment and wiring faulty. Again the thoughtless disposal of whey can lead to pollution. It is important to consider every aspect of the process before embarking on a commercial venture.

THE CHEESE REGULATIONS 1970 (S.I. No. 94) & Amendment 1974 (S.I. No. 1122).

These regulations are of interest to all cheesemakers whether they intend to sell their product or not. The non-seller will find that the definitions of types of cheese, and the composition of the various varieties will help to explain the differences in recipes and procedures. For the cheesemaker with selling in mind, it is vital that the regulations are read, understood, and complied with. They lay down precise specifications for the composition, ingredients, labelling, and advertisement of all cheese manufactured.

There are several definitions which are important: *Cheese* is the fresh or matured product of the coagulation of milk and the subsequent partial draining of whey. No source of milk is specified and it is therefore, by inference, the milk of any animal, likely or unlikely. This means that cheese made from the product of any lactation is subject to these regulations.

Soft Cheese means cheese which is readily deformed by moderate pressure, and includes cream cheese and curd cheese.

Hard Cheese means cheese other than soft cheese. Descriptions such as semi-soft and semi-hard are frequently used in other texts, but they do not occur in the regulations.

Sell includes an offer or exposure for sale, or to have in possession for sale. In the case of cheese which is offered as a sandwich filling or with or after a meal, if the cheese is described by variety or classification, it must comply with the requirements of that description. It is worthwhile mentioning here that any home-made cheese that is included in food offered to customers in a café or paying guests in the house must have been prepared under those conditions covered under the Food Regulations referred to earlier.

Starter means a living culture of lactic acid producing bacteria.

There are other definitions which are concerned with cheese spread, whey cheese, processed cheese, etc., which will need to be referred to if it is the intention of the cheesemaker to produce any of these for sale.

Composition and description

Hard Cheese. The common, named varieties of hard cheese are listed in Schedule 1 of the Regulations, and if such cheeses are made for sale and marketed under their particular varietal names, their composition must comply with the specification for that particular variety in regard to milk fat and water content.

The English cheeses mentioned in Schedule 1 are as follows:

Variety of Cheese	Minimum % of Milk Fat in the DRY MATTER	Maximum % of Water in the total Weight of Cheese
Cheddar	48	39
Blue Stilton	48	42
Derby	48	42
Leicester	48	42
Cheshire	48	44
Dunlop	48	44
Gloucester	48	44
Double Gloucester	48	44
Caerphilly	48	46
Wensleydale	48	46
White Stilton	48	46
Lancashire	48	48

If a hard cheese is made, either of an un-named variety, or of a variety known, but not listed in Schedule 1 of the regulations, retail sales of such a cheese must be accompanied by an appropriate description thus:

1. *Full fat hard cheese* — If the cheese contains not less that 48% milk fat in the dry matter and not more than 48% water (in the total weight of the cheese).

2. *Medium fat hard cheese* — If the cheese contains less than 48% and not less than 10% milk fat in the dry matter and not more than 48% water (in the total weight of the cheese).

3. *Skimmed milk hard cheese* — If the cheese contains less than 10% milk fat in the dry matter and not more than 48% water (in the total weight of cheese).

Alternatively the cheese must bear a declaration of a prescribed format which contains either

1) the minimum percentage milk fat content in the dry matter and the maximum percentage water content (in the total weight of cheese).

or 2) the minimum percentage milk fat content (in the total weight of cheese).

It is important to notice that there is a difference between the 'percentage milk fat in the dry matter' and 'percentage milk fat'. The words in brackets, 'in the total weight of cheese' do not appear in the text of the regulations, but have been added here to emphasise the difference. In order to avoid confusion between the two terms, it is important to remember that, despite the draining of the curd to expel whey, a considerable amount of water remains in the finished cheese, and that although the cheesemaker endeavours to retain as much of the total milk solids as possible, there is always some loss to the whey.

Therefore the '% fat in the total weight of cheese' refers to that proportion of the curd, both total solids and water, which is fat and the '% fat in the dry matter' to that proportion of the curd solids, excluding the water, which is fat.

The various labellings which comply with the regulations give the producer of a known variety of hard cheese four alternatives. For example, a Lancashire cheese, provided it conforms to the specification laid down in Schedule 1 could be labelled:

  a) Lancashire Cheese
  b) Full fat hard cheese
  c) 48% fat in dry matter and 48% water
or d) 25% fat cheese.

Soft Cheese. None of the well known soft cheeses are listed by name in the regulations with their accompanying specifications. Therefore the maker of the soft cheese for sale must comply with labelling requirements similar to those for unlisted hard cheese, which are based on the fat and water content. These are as follows:

1) Full fat soft cheese — If the cheese contains not less than 20% milk fat and not more than 60% water (in the total weight of cheese).

2) Medium fat soft cheese — If the cheese contains less than 20% but not less than 10% milk fat and not more than 70% water (in the total weight of cheese).

3) Low fat soft cheese — If the cheese contains less than 10% but not less than 2% milk fat and not more than 80% water (in the total weight of cheese).

4) Skimmed milk soft cheese — If the cheese contains less than 2% milk fat and not more than 80% water (in the total weight of cheese).

Additionally, soft cheese described as *Cream Cheese* shall contain not less than 45% milk fat in the total weight of cheese and *Double Cream Cheese* shall contain not less than 65% milk fat in the total weight of cheese.

Although the water content of soft cheese is considerably higher than that of hard, the fat content of full fat, medium fat, and low fat cheese whether hard or soft is not very different when expressed in similar terms, and it is unclear in the regulations why total weight percentages are preferred for soft cheeses and dry matter percentages for hard cheeses.

Permitted ingredients. The regulations tightly control the ingredients for cheesemaking. The home cheesemaker is unlikely to use any additive other than starter, rennet, salt, and sometimes colouring, and blue or white moulds, all of which are permitted. The addition of sage and green vegetable colouring to Sage Derby is also permitted. There are various other additives, such as emulsifiers, stabilisers, and antioxidants which are permitted within strictly controlled limits, but these are usually only of interest in large scale commercial production, and particularly in the production of processed cheese and cheese spread.

From the small scale producer's point of view, the major difficulty in complying with the regulations regarding the labelling and composition of cheese is the difficulty and expense in getting the cheese analysed, and this is the only way of being sure that the cheese is actually of the standard stated on the label. Ideally each cheese or batch of cheeses should be analysed separately, as a drop in the quality of the milk or an accident of mishandling can drop a 'borderline' full fat cheese into the medium fat bracket. It is also significant to point out that a medium fat label on a full fat cheese is equally misleading to the purchaser and therefore in breach of the regulations. Fortunately, the texture of hard cheese is a good guide to its composition, and the legal composition is not difficult to achieve with good milk and careful cheesemaking practice. Soft cheese is more difficult to assess, and it is the water content more than the fat content that the soft cheesemakers will have to watch carefully.

Finally there are legal requirements for any business, including cheesemaking for sale, in respect of insurance, rating, planning, and taxation which must be complied with, and the advice of the appropriate authority should be sought before embarking on any commercial venture, however small.

Persons considering large scale production, and in particular registered milk producers, are subject to further regulations with regard to quantity of production and grading of cheese for sale and should consult the Milk Marketing Board.

PART TWO
<u>CHEESES</u>

CHEESES

THE RECIPES which follow are mostly proven, established methods of making named varieties of cheese. This does not mean that they are the only recipes for making cheese. Many variations are possible. A slight difference in scalding temperature, acid development, or curd handling can produce a completely new cheese which can be called 'Fred's Cheese' or 'Home Farm Cheese' or any other original name the maker chooses. If it tastes good and looks good, it is good cheese, unless it is for resale, in which case of course, it must comply with the regulations and grading standards.

The number of soft cheese recipes included is limited. Many books are available which will guide and help the soft cheese maker. Most of them are good; many of them are excellent. The hard cheese recipes have all been tried and proven before inclusion. Whether they are accurate representations of a classic variety of cheese is debatable. It is difficult today to produce a classic cheese. For instance, Dunlop cheese was produced from the milk of Ayrshire cows, fed solely on Ayrshire pastures, with hay and roots and perhaps a little grain for winter feeding. Today the milk is almost certain to be from Friesian cows on seeded and fertilised pastures who are fed nationally produced cake in the parlour, and silage with additives throughout the winter. The quality and flavour of the milk determines the authenticity of the cheese, but the cheesemaker determines the difference between one cheese and another. With milk from the same cows on the same feed at any time of year, it is possible by using guideline instructions to produce an impressive variety of cheeses, or simply to regularly make one variety of cheese which is acceptable to the people who are to eat it.

SOFT CHEESES

ACID CURD CHEESE

The simplest form of soft cheese is acid curd cheese. This is made by assisting the natural souring and coagulating process by a strong inoculation of cheese starter bacteria. It can be made with whole milk, with part skimmed milk, or with left-over starter.

Adjust the temperature of the milk to 90°F, 32°C.

Add Starter. 10 tablespoons (150mls) per gallon. Leave for 12 to 24 hours until the curd is firm and the whey has begun to rise.

Pour the curd or ladle it into a clean coarse cloth suspended over a bucket or sink. Draw the corners of the cloth together to form a bag and suspend over the bucket to drain.

Scrape the curd from the cloth occasionally during draining to unblock the weave.

After 24 to 48 hours the curd should be drained sufficiently to be removed from the cloth and whilst still moist should show no visible whey.

Add salt or other flavouring to taste.

Pack into pots or wrap in film and store in a refrigerator. This cheese should be used within 7 — 10 days.

The addition of rennet to the inoculated milk produces a quicker coagulation and a less acid cheese which can be bag drained or molded or a combination of both.

MOULDED SIMPLE CURD or COULOMMIER CHEESE

A Coulommier is traditionally round, about 5" diameter and 2" high with reed patterning on the top and bottom, but the same cheese will mold well in many shapes and sizes. It can also be 'striped' by adding Annato to a portion of the milk before renneting and ladling uncoloured and coloured curd into the mold in layers. Herbed cheese is made by adding green vegetable colouring and crushed herbs in place of the Annatto.

Adjust the temperature of the milk to 90°F, 32°C.

Add starter. 2.5mls (½ teaspoon) per gallon and stir in

thoroughly.

Add rennet. 3mls per gallon diluted in cold water and stir well in. Top stir until coagulation begins. Leave for 1—1½ hours until a firm curd has formed.

Ladle in thin slices into a mold standing on a mat and board on a drainer. The mold can be topped up as the curd sinks.

Leave to drain for 12 to 24 hours. Turn onto a clean mat and board and leave until the mold can be easily lifted away. If a double mold is used, the top ring can be removed before the first turning, and more frequent turning thereafter will speed up the draining process.

Sprinkle salt on both surfaces of the cheese and leave in a warm place for a few hours for the surface to dry.

Store in a refrigerator.

This cheese should be used within 7 — 10 days.

Cream Cheeses

A typical cream cheese is a soft unripened cheese with rich, mildly acid flavour. It has a granular, buttery texture and a creamy appearance. There are two recognised varieties:

Cream Cheese and
Double Cream Cheese

CREAM CHEESE (single cream)

This variety is sometimes described as renneted cream cheese. It is made from good quality cream with a butterfat content of 20 — 25%. Two pints of cream will yield approximately six 4-oz cheeses.

Adjust the temperature to 75°F, 24°C.

Add starter. 5mls to every 2 pints cream, and leave to ripen for 2 — 3 hours.

Add Rennet. 2mls diluted in 6 times the volume of water per 2 pints. Stir thoroughly and stand for 8 — 12 hours to coagulate.

Ladle the formed curd in thick slices into a course cloth which has been scalded and cooled before use. Gather together the corners of the cloth and hang the bag in a cool (50° — 55°F, 10° — 13°C) well ventilated place to drain. Alternatively place the bag of curd between two boards on a draining rack and put a 1—2lb weight on top to exert pressure.

Open the cloth at 2 — 4 hour intervals. Scrape the curd down and mix well with a clean knife. The more often this is done the quicker the cheese will drain. The cloth can be changed if the mesh becomes clogged.

When draining ceases tip the curd into a bowl, mix well and add ¼oz dry salt to each quart of cream used.

Fill into molds or containers. The traditional cream cheese molds are of 4oz capacity, mounted in groups on a metal base. Before filling, line the molds with greaseproof paper leaving sufficient at each end to fold over when removed from mold. Plastic pots with lids are more frequently used nowadays. This cheese may be stored in a refrigerator for up to a week.

DOUBLE CREAM CHEESE

Double cream cheese should be produced from cream containing 50—59% butterfat. The cream is raised to 75°F, 24°C and starter added as described for single cream cheese.

Double cream drains without the addition of rennet and merely needs to be ladled or poured into a linen cloth for drainage. Some makers prefer to add salt to the cream before draining rather than to the drained curd. The treatment during and after draining should be the same as for single cream cheese, although drainage may take a little longer.

A quart of cream of the appropriate fat content will yield about eight 4oz double cream cheeses. Double cream cheese is thus richer in butterfat than single cream cheese, but does not keep quite as long.

The methods of molding, packing, storage and marketing need not differ in any respect from those described for single cream cheese.

COLWICK CHEESE

This is a round cheese with a hollow centre. This hollow can be filled with whipped cream and fruit or with herbs and chopped vegetables in sour cream.

Adjust the temperature of the milk to 90°F, 32°C.

Add starter. 1.5mls per gallon and stir well.

Add rennet. 5mls per gallon. Stir thoroughly for 2 minutes and top stir until coagulation begins. Leave approximately 1 hour until a firm curd has formed.

Line a mold with a cheesecloth just large enough to completely line the mold and hang over the sides. Too big a cloth makes an unwieldy bundle.

Ladle the curd in thin slices into the cloth lined mold standing on a board and fold the corners over the top of the curd. Leave to drain for 2 hours.

Draw the four corners of the cloth together and tie in a 'Stilton Knot' (holding three corners of the cloth in one hand, turn the fourth corner of the cloth round the other three and knot it upon itself), gently pulling the curd away from the sides of the mold. Leave the knot centrally placed on the surface of the curd to cause the hollow. Leave for 24 hours, tightening the knot periodically. Turn the cheese in the mold onto a clean board with the knot at the bottom and leave until sufficiently drained.

Remove the cheese from the mold and cloth and turn with the hollow on top.

Add salt if required by lightly sprinkling it on the surface.

Store in a refrigerator.

This cheese should be used within 7 — 10 days.

PONT L'EVEQUE

This is a small flat oblong cheese about 5" x 3" x 2". It can be eaten fresh or matured for up to 5 weeks when it will develop a soft runny centre.

Adjust the temperature of the milk to 90°F, 32°C.

Add starter. 1.5mls per gallon and stir well in.

Add rennet. 3.5mls per gallon, stir thoroughly for two minutes and top stir until coagulation begins. Leave for approximately 1 hour until a curd forms.

Ladle the curd in thin slices onto a course cloth spread over a drainer. Fold over the ends of the cloth and leave in a warm place for 15 minutes.

Cut the curd with a knife into blocks about 3" square to assist drainage and leave a further 15 minutes.

Bundle the curd into a Stilton Knot and leave until the curd has a flakey, not gritty, texture, tightening the knot every 15 minutes.

Crumble the curd and pack carefully into the mold standing on a mat and board.

Add salt by sprinkling between the layers of curd at molding, approximately 1 teaspoonful per gallon of milk used.

Turn as soon as the mold is full onto a clean mat and board.

Turn daily for approximately 3 days until the cheese will easily leave the mold.

Scrape the surface with a hot knife to seal any cracks.

Cheese for eating fresh should be kept in the refrigerator and used within 10 days.

Cheese for ripening should be moved to the storage area, turned daily for 10 days and weekly thereafter.

TRADITIONAL COTTAGE CHEESE

This cheese is usually made from separated or skimmed milk.

Adjust the temperature of the milk to 70°F, 21°C.

Add starter. 30mls (2 tablespoons) per gallon.

Add rennet. Approximately 1ml per gallon diluted in 40 times its volume of cold water.

Stir for 10 minutes.

Leave for 12 to 16 hours.

Cut into ¾" cubes and stir gently for 5 minutes being careful not to damage the curd.

Raise the temperature gradually to 98°F, 37°C, taking 30 — 40 minutes in the process and gently stirring occasionally.

Drain through a course cloth — either 'bag' draining or on a draining rack.

Turn the drained curd into a bowl.

Add salt. 1oz per gallon of milk used.

Pack into cartons or tubs.

Store in the refrigerator.

Use within 10 days.

Flavourings such as chives, pineapple, ham, shrimps, etc. can be added at the salting stage.

The true Brie or Camembert can only be made in the regions of France where they originate. The milk, the moulds, the maturing conditions are all an essential part of the cheese. However a very good imitation can be made in the home, provided it is made with care. It will be necessary to purchase a Camembert mould culture from a suitable supplier and make it up according to the instructions.

BRIE
Adjust the temperature of the milk to 86°F, 30°C.
Add starter. 4 drops per gallon. Stir well in.
Add Camembert type mould culture. 5mls (1 teaspoon) per gallon. Stir well in.
Add rennet. 1.5mls per gallon. Stir thoroughly and leave to coagulate.
Cut into ½" cubes, both ways with a vertical knife and one way with a horizontal knife.
Pitch for 10 minutes.
Draw the whey and then ladle the drained curd into Brie molds placed on mats and boards.
Leave to drain. As the curd settles into the mold, more can be added until the ring is full.
Turn as soon as the curd is firm enough onto a clean mat and board.
Rub a little salt gently into the surfaces at turning.
Turn the cheese frequently to assist draining until the mold can be removed without the cheese losing shape.
This cheese should be ripened for up to 6 weeks in a well ventilated store at a temperature of 15°C, 59°F turning daily. It is not advisable to ripen this cheese with other cheese as the characteristic white mould will become contaminated.

CAMEMBERT
There are two methods for producing a Camembert type cheese: seeded where the mould is used instead of starter, and sprayed, where the mould is sprayed onto the surface of a drained curd cheese.

Seeded

Adjust the temperature of the milk to 85°F, 29°C.

Add Camembert mould (made up to the manufacturer's instructions) at the rate of 5 mls (1 teaspoon) per gallon. Stir thoroughly.

Add rennet. 1.5mls per gallon in 6 times the volume of cold water. Leave to form curd.

Ladle the curd in even slices into molds placed on mats and boards.

When the curd has sunk to halfway down the mold, invert carefully and sprinkle a little salt on the surfaces.

Turn frequently until the mold can be safely removed without the cheese losing shape.

Dry the surface carefully. The proper development of the white mould depends on the surface being dry and uncontaminated so that the desired mould takes precedence over any other. The surface of the molded cheese must either be patted dry with clean sterile cloths until no moisture escapes, or better still dried in a warm draught. A hair dryer or fan heater can be used to speed up the surface drying. The cheese should then be carefully protected from dust and insects during the maturing period of 2 — 6 weeks, the correct maturing temperature being 59°F, 15°C.

Sprayed

Adjust the temperature of the milk to 85°F, 29°C.

Add starter. Two drops per gallon. Do not add too much starter or an acid, dry cheese will result.

Add rennet. 1.5mls per gallon in 6 times the volume of cold water. Stir thoroughly.

Proceed as for seeded cheese until the cheese is removed from the molds.

Dry the surface of the cheese very thoroughly. If necessary, leave in a warm place until a coat has begun to form.

Spray with a mist spray of Camembert mould prepared by adding 5ml of culture made up to the manufacturer's instructions to a further 100mls of cool boiled water. A spray of the kind supplied for the treatment of house plants is ideal for this purpose, but if a spray is not available, the mould solution can be applied to the surface of the cheese with a small soft paint brush.

After coating, the cheese must be carefully air dried before maturing for 2 — 6 weeks.

===

SEMI-HARD CHEESES

Legally this category does not exist. It is a term loosely applied to unpressed or lightly pressed cheeses, but does not necessarily describe the texture of the finished product. Home cheesemakers can make the following cheeses without using a press, such pressures as may be required being applied by piling weights or other heavy objects on top of the follower. For guidance 'light pressure' over a 6" diameter cheese will require the addition of 7 — 10lbs of weights. Medium pressure will be 10 — 30lbs; and maximum, as much as can reasonably be piled on.

SMALLHOLDER or AMERICAN FARMHOUSE CHEESE

Adjust the temperature of the milk to 90°F, 32°C.

Add starter. 30mls (2 tablespoons) per gallon. Leave for 45 minutes.

Add rennet. 2.5mls per gallon diluted in cold water. Stir in well and top stir until coagulation begins. Leave approximately 45 minutes until a firm curd is formed.

Cut the curd into ½" cubes, being careful not to damage the curd.

Raise the temperature to 100°F, 38°C gradually over a period of 30 minutes, by which time the cubes should have shrunk and be fairly firm to handle.

Pitch or allow to settle for 5 minutes.

Pour the curd carefully into a cloth held firmly over a bucket or sink.

Remove the bundle of curd from the whey and tie in a Stilton Knot. Place on a drainer.

Tighten the knot every 10 minutes for the next hour, being careful to keep the curd warm and out of the whey.

Mill when a rubbery texture has been reached into pieces about 1".

Add salt. ⅓oz per gallon milk used.

Pack into a mold lined with damp cheesecloth. Put on a follower and apply light pressure for 2—4 hours.

Remove from the mold and turn into a clean dry cloth.

Return to press increasing up to medium pressure.

Turn daily into clean cloths for two more days using muslin cloths on the last day.

Remove from the mold and grease well with lard or solid vegetable fat. For a smooth finish return to press without a cloth and with a thin flat follower for a further 2—4 hours.

Put to store. This cheese will benefit from a supporting bandage for the first week in store. Cut a strip of cloth the same width as the height of the cheese and slightly longer than the distance round the circumference. Fix tightly round the cheese and join with a needle and thread or by waxing the ends together.

Turn daily for the first week and every 3 days thereafter.

This is a mild cheese with limited keeping qualities and is ready for use in 4—6 weeks.

Faults in smallholder cheese

Any mould which grows on the surface of the cheese can be wiped away, but care must be taken not to damage the skin. Cracks in the skin — usually caused by incorrect storage conditions — must be filled with fat before moulds can enter the body of the cheese.

A 'slumped' or misshapen cheese is usually the result of too moist a curd or not turning regularly. The support bandage will help to prevent slumping, but the turning must be done *at least* daily for the first week.

LITTLE DUTCH TYPE of cheese

Adjust the temperature of the milk to 90°F, 32°C.

Add starter. 90 mls (6 tablespoons) per gallon.

Add Annatto. 2.5 mls (½ teaspoon) per gallon. Stir thoroughly into the milk.

Add rennet. 2.5 mls (½ teaspoon) per gallon diluted in 6 times the volume of cold water.

Stir for 3 minutes.

Leave for 30 minutes for a fairly firm curd to form.

Cut the curd into ¼" cubes. Stir gently for 5 minutes taking care not to damage the curd.

Raise the temperature of the curds and whey to 105°F, 41°C, taking 30-40 minutes in the process and stirring carefully throughout.

Pitch for 5 minutes.

Drain the curd through a cloth over a bucket and return the curd to the vessel. Retain the whey.

Add salt. ½ oz per gallon and mix well.

Pack the curd into a mold, warmed and lined with a hot damp cloth. Put on a follower.

Press lightly for ten minutes.

Turn the cheese into a fresh cloth and dip the whole into the whey. Return to the press.

Repeat the turning and dipping twice more at 20 minute intervals. Leave overnight.

Next day. Turn the cheese into a hot dry cloth and return to press with medium pressure for a further 24 hours.

Remove from mold and leave to dry on a mat and board in a warm dry place for two to three days turning regularly. When the rind is quite dry, coat with cheese wax and put to store.

This cheese should have a clean, mild flavour and a smooth surface. It is ready to use in 3-4 weeks.

Faults in Little Dutch Cheese

Patchy colouring is caused by adding the Annatto when the acidity has begun to develop, or by inadequate mixing. Underdeveloped flavour is caused by the curd having become chilled. Mould growth between the wax and the rind of the cheese is caused by waxing a damp cheese, or by pinholes in the wax. The wax must be hot enough to flow round the cheese, and the cheese must not be so cold at waxing that the wax solidifies before it has time to fully cover the surface.

STILTON CHEESE

Adjust the temperature of the milk to 85°F, 29°C.

Add starter. 1-2 mls per gallon, the higher level being used for milk straight from the udder. (Too much starter will give an over-acid, chalky cheese.) Mix well in.

Add rennet. 1.5 mls per gallon mixed with 6 times the volume of cold water. Stir for 3-5 minutes and leave for 90 minutes to form a firm curd.

There are two methods of transferring the curd to the cloth.

Either ladle into coarse cloths in uniformly thin slices as quickly as possible without damaging the curd.

Or cut both ways with a vertical knife into pillars, approximately ½" square. Allow the cut curd to pitch for 5 minutes, draw off the surface whey and carefully transfer the settled curd to the cloths.

Fold the corners of the cloths across the curd as it lies in the vessel, and allow the whey to collect round the bundle for an hour.

Draw off the whey and stand for a further 1 hour allowing the whey to collect round the bundle again.

Now draw off the whey again, tie the bundle of curd in a Stilton Knot and place on a draining rack.

Tighten the bundle at hourly intervals until the curd is firm and the acidity has developed sufficiently.

Turn the curd carefully out of the cloth into the vessel and cut into cubes about 3" square which will stand on their own. Turn the blocks occasionally until the texture becomes flaky. This curd can be milled, salted, and molded once it has reached an acidity of 4.5 or left to develop an acidity of up to 9.0, but it is most important that it is molded before becoming too firm or too dry, and the best time to mold will depend far more on the texture of the curd than on the acidity.

Mill into pieces about 1" square.

Add salt. 1 oz per 2½ lbs curd (2½ gallons of milk used), mix thoroughly and allow the salt to dissolve before packing.

Pack into molds WITHOUT cloths and lay a follower or flat disc on the top. Do not apply any weight or pressure. Cover the entire mold with a damp cloth.

Turn in the mold every day (in hot condition twice daily) and rewrap in a clean damp cloth. It is essential that the outside of the cheese remains moist.

Remove from the mold when the cheese has shrunk sufficiently to slide easily in the mold (4-6 days).

Scrape the surface with a knife dipped in hot water until all surface cracks are filled.

Cover with a dry cloth and keep in a warm dry place for the surface to seal over.

Put to store. If the storage area is insufficiently humid, cover with a damp cloth to prevent the skin cracking. White Stilton is ready to use in three weeks.

BLUE STILTON is made in the same manner, the blue mould, which should be a commercially produced culture, being added to the milk before renneting or mixed with a little whey and poured over the curd at milling. After a few weeks in storage the Blue Stilton should be pierced with a fine steel needle from top to bottom and from side to side several times to allow air to enter and assist the mould growth. This cheese will take at least four to six months to reach maturity.

Acidities

Milk at renneting	0.17 to 0.19%
Whey at drawing	0.12
Whey at tying up	0.15
Whey at turning out	0.19 to 0.20
Curd at milling	0.35 to 0.90 (depending on the texture of the curd.)

White Stilton should not exceed a maximum acidity of 0.55%

Faults in Stilton

Too dry a curd at molding gives a cheese which does not bond and has gaps between the pieces of curd too big to fill on scraping. This will yield a dry hard cheese subject to cheese mites.

Slip coat is a slimy condition of the coat which can flow off, allowing the body of the cheese to bulge out of the gaps. This is usually caused by bad storage conditions. The broken coat can be scraped off and new coat encouraged by dusting the patches with rice flour or purified chalk.

Restricted mould growth in a blue cheese is due to lack of air in the cheese. More thorough needling is necessary.

A *dry blue cheese* is usually immature, provided that the curd was moist enough on packing. If a cheese has been cut too soon, it is possible, with care, to work up a surface with a knife and hot water on the cut face and return the cheese to store for a further maturing period.

═══════════════════════════════

HARD CHEESES

A hard cheese is one which is made from 'worked' curd which has been pressed in the mold to consolidate the curd and to produce a cheese of the moisture content required for the variety being made (see Chapter 5). It is important that the curd attains the right texture before milling, and the home cheesemaker will soon learn to judge the stage of development by look, feel, and smell.

The ideal acidities for each stage in the production of the varieties of cheese which follow are given at the end of the individual instructions for the benefit of those cheesemakers working with an acid meter. It may appear confusing that the acidity of the milk at renneting is higher than that of the whey at cutting the curd. This is a natural part of the enzyme action and is perfectly normal. Once the curd is cut, the acidity will begin to rise again, and provided the procedure is followed carefully, should continue to rise steadily until the desired level is reached.

CAERPHILLY CHEESE

Adjust the temperature of the milk to 70°F, 21°C.

Add starter. 75 mls (5 tablespoons) per gallon. Gradually raise the temperature of the milk to 90°F, 32° taking 1 to 2½ hours.

Add rennet. 1 ml per gallon, stir well and leave to form a firm curd for approximately 40 minutes.

Cut the curd both ways with the vertical knife followed by both ways with the horizontal knife into cubes approximately ¼" square.

Stir for 10 to 15 minutes.

Raise the temperature of the curd to 94°F, 34°C stirring all the time taking 35-40 minutes in the process.

Pitch for 10-15 minutes.

Push the curd towards the back of the vat and run off the whey. Shape the curd into cone-shaped piles and then cut into wedge-shaped pieces. Pile these wedges at the back of the vat and cover with a cloth to keep warm. After about an hour, when the curd is firm and silky, remove one block at a time and cut into 1" squares with a sharp knife.

Add salt. ⅛ oz per gallon of milk and pack whilst the curd is still warm into a mold lined with a warm damp cloth.

Apply light pressure, just enough to consolidate the curd. After two hours turn the cheese into a clean warm damp cloth and return to press with medium pressure.

Next day remove the cheese and put for 24 hours into a brine bath. Brine is prepared by adding salt, approximately 2 lbs per gallon, to boiled, cooled water. The cheese will float in this. Too strong or too weak a solution will spoil the coat of the cheese.

Remove the cheese from the bath and put to drain in a cool, airy place for several hours before putting into store.

This cheese is ready for use in 3 weeks.

Acidities

At renneting	0.20 to 0.23%
At cutting	0.13 to 0.16
At pitching	0.15 to 0.18
At molding	0.21 to 0.28

Faults in Caerphilly

A slimy coat is usually caused by too weak a brine bath or by putting to store before the cheese has dried on all surfaces. A cracked coat can be caused by bad storage conditions or by too strong a brine bath.

CHEDDAR CHEESE

Adjust the temperature of the milk to 85°F, 29°C and maintain this temperature until scalding.

Add starter. 35-40 mls (2½ tablespoons) per gallon (NB. In cold conditions this inoculation can be increased up to twice the quantity). Leave for 30-45 minutes.

Add rennet. 1.5 mls per gallon in four times the volume of cold water. Stir thoroughly, and top stir until coagulation begins. Leave for 40-45 minutes until a firm curd has formed.

Cut the curd into small cubes, both ways with the vertical knife followed by both ways with the horizontal knife, being careful not to damage the curd.

Raise the temperature of the curds and whey to 100°F, 38°C over a period of 30-40 minutes, stirring gently all the time to prevent the curd particles sticking together. Remove from the heat source.

Pitch or allow to settle for approximately 10 minutes. The pitching time can be increased if the acidity is developing at a slower rate than is required.

Push up the mass of curd to one end of the vat using the hand or a suitable board.

Draw the whey from the curd without disturbing the consolidating mass. The small particles of curd caught in the strainer should be returned to the mass before they get cool.

Cut the block of curd, as soon as most of the whey is drawn, into strips about 2" wide down the length of the vessel. Pile the central slices on top of those nearest the vessel sides to create a channel for the whey. Cover the blocks with a cloth to keep warm. Leave for 15 minutes removing the whey as it accumulates.

Cheddaring is the process of cutting or pulling the strips of curd apart at intervals, removing the whey and restacking the curd with the top strips at the bottom of the stack and the bottom strips at the top. Do this every 15-20 minutes for 1½ to 2 hours until very little whey is draining from the curd.

The texture of the curd will have changed to that of thick rubber. It will be stretchy, look silky, tear rather than break, and give off a distinctly cheesey smell.

Mill the curd into pieces approximately ¾" diameter.

Add salt. 1 oz per 4 lbs curd (4 gallons of milk) and mix well.

Pack the curd into a mold lined with a damp cheesecloth, fold the ends of the cloth over the curd and put on the follower.

Press with medium pressure for approximately 4-8 hours.

Turn the cheese into a clean damp cloth and return to press at maximum pressure.

Turn daily into a clean dry cloth for three more days all at maximum pressure.

Remove from the press, rub well with lard, butter, or solid vegetable fat and return to the press without a cloth, with a well fitting flat follower for a further 4 hours to give a good finish to the coat.

Remove from the press and allow to dry in a cool well ventilated place for 12-24 hours.

Put to store turning daily for the first week and weekly thereafter.

With careful storage Cheddar cheese can be matured for up to 18 months, although there will be noticeable loss of weight in the long matured cheese. The smaller homemade cheeses of 4-6 lbs appear to reach an acceptable maturity sooner than the larger cheeses and a 4 lb cheddar made to this recipe gives a mild but acceptable cheese at 4-6 weeks, a more flavoursome cheese at 6-8 weeks and a very acceptable flavour at up to 6 months. It is debatable whether the improved flavour justifies the loss of weight on maturing for over 6 months. The cheesemaker must decide this for him or herself.

Acidities

At starting	0.14 to 0.16%
At renneting	0.19 to 0.21
At cutting	0.14 to 0.16
At pitching	0.17 to 0.2
At drawing whey	0.21 to 0.23
At milling	0.75 to 0.85

Faults in Cheddar Cheese

Cracked rinds, usually due to poor storage conditions. The cracks must be filled with grease and the cheese watched carefully for signs of mould penetration. If this should occur, the cheese should be used immediately.

Loose texture is usually caused by not working the curd sufficiently or by insufficient pressure.

An uneven coat is often caused by the skin drying in the mold before taking up a smooth shape. If on turning on the second day in the press the cheese has not got a smooth even coat, it should be dipped for 30 seconds in water at 130°F, 54°C and returned to full pressure in a clean, smooth, dry cloth.

Gassy or 'blown' cheese is caused by contamination. More attention must be paid to hygiene and general cleanliness and the starter should be checked for possible contaminants. Check also the quality of the milk.

CHESHIRE CHEESE

Adjust the temperature of the milk to 85°F, 29°C.

Add starter. 75 mls (5 tablespoons) per gallon. Stir thoroughly. Leave for 30-35 minutes.

Add rennet. 1.5 mls per gallon in 4 times the volume of cold water. Stir thoroughly. Then top stir until coagulation begins. Cover and keep warm. Leave for 30-35 minutes until a firm curd has formed.

Cut the curd both ways with the vertical knives and lengthwise only with the horizontal knife, being careful not to damage the curd.

Raise the temperature of the curds and whey to 94°F, 34°C over a period of 30 minutes, stirring very gently all the time. This curd is very soft and must be handled carefully to avoid damage. Remove from the heat source.

Pitch or allow to settle for 30 minutes or until the curd particles, whilst still soft, retain their shape on being squeezed.

Draw the whey from the curd without disturbing the consolidating mass. The small particles of curd caught in the strainer should be returned to the mass before they get cool.

Cut the curd into blocks approximately 4" square and stack at the sides of the vessel leaving a channel for the whey. Cover and leave for 20 minutes, removing the whey as it accumulates.

Break the blocks by hand (cutting tends to seal the edges and impair drainage) and restack, top blocks to the bottom of the stack and bottom blocks on the top every 20 minutes for the next 1-1½ hours, periodically clearing the whey. Keep warm throughout this process. After 4-6 breaks the curd should be firm, dry and be of a leafy texture.

Add salt ¼ oz per gallon of milk used, by sprinkling over the blocks of curd.

Mill the curd into pieces about ¾".

Pack the curd into molds lined with a damp cheesecloth, packing down firmly to consolidate the curd.

Leave without pressure for 2 hours.

Turn into a damp cloth and return to the mold. Apply medium pressure. Leave overnight.

Turn into a smooth clean dry cloth and return to press applying maximum pressure.

Turn daily for 3 days keeping maximum pressure throughout and using a fine cloth on the last day in the press.

Remove from the press and grease well with lard, butter or vegetable fat.

Keep in a cool well ventilated place for 8 hours.

Put to store turning daily for the first week and weekly thereafter.

This cheese is ready for use in 3-6 weeks. The early ripening cheese will have a slightly acid flavour and a moist texture. A well made Cheshire can be matured for up to 4 months when it will be smoother flavoured and creamier in texture.

Acidities

At renneting	0.18 to 0.19%
At cutting	0.12 to 0.13
At pitching	0.15 to 0.155
At drawing whey	0.16 to 0.17
At first break	0.2 to 0.25
At milling	0.6 to 0.65

Faults in Cheshire Cheese

Over acid flavour is usually caused by over 'ripening' of the milk before renneting.

Too hard a texture can be caused by using milk of insufficient fat content, cutting the curd too small, damaging the curd badly during cutting and scalding at too high a temperature.

Too wet a cheese can be caused by allowing the curds to chill and so interrupting the drainage, poor handling technique, or not draining the curd blocks sufficiently before pressing.

A misshapen cheese is usually the result of bad pressing, not turning daily in store, or unsuitable storage conditions.

A mottled or discoloured inner cheese is usually caused by contamination. Check hygiene, general cleanliness, the quality of the milk and the starter.

DERBY CHEESE

Adjust the temperature of the milk to 70°F, 21°C.

Add starter. 75 mls (5 tablespoons) per gallon. Stir thoroughly.

Raise the temperature of the milk to 85°F, 29°C and leave for 30-45 minutes.

Add rennet. 1.5 ml per gallon. Stir thoroughly and top stir until coagulation begins. Leave for 45 minutes until a firm curd has formed.

Cut the curd lengthwise and crosswise with the vertical knife and lengthwise only with the horizontal knife.

Pitch for 5 minutes.

Raise the temperature of the curds and whey to 95°F, 35°C over a period of 50 minutes stirring gently all the time.

Pitch for 10-20 minutes.

Draw the whey from the curd as quickly as possible.

Cut the curd into 4" blocks and pile down the sides of the vessel.

Recut and pile at 20 minute intervals over the next 2-3 hours. *The texture* of the curd should then be leafy but still very moist.

Mill in ½" pieces.

Add salt. ¼ oz per gallon of milk used. Mix thoroughly into the moist curd.

Pack into molds lined with damp cloths and apply just enough pressure to cause the whey to run freely. Leave for 6-8 hours.

Turn into clean damp cloths and return to press with medium pressure.

Next day turn twice during the day into clean DRY cloths. Return to press keeping medium pressure throughout.

Remove from the press and keep for 24 hours in a cool well ventilated place.

Put to store after greasing with lard, butter, or vegetable fat. A support bandage for the first 3-4 days will help to keep the shape of the cheese.

Turn daily for the first week and twice weekly thereafter.

This is a mild smooth cheese which can be used from 4-12 weeks after making. It is not usually improved by maturing for any longer than three months.

SAGE DERBY is made as above, but a third of the curd is separated out at whey drawing and mixed with green colouring (which can be made by liquidising and straining spinach, cabbage, or other green vegetables) to which has been added some finely chopped young sage leaves. On packing, a third plain curd is followed by a third coloured curd and the final layer of plain curd.

Acidities

At renneting	0.20%
At pitching	0.20 to 0.22
At milling	0.60 to 0.75

Faults in Derby Cheese

This is a moist cheese and therefore susceptible to contamination in store.

Damaged coats must be filled with fat immediately or mould growth will penetrate.

A *sour cheese* can be caused by incorrect scalding.

A *dry cheese* is usually caused by low fat milk or fat loss at cutting the curd.

DORSET CHEESE

This cheese is made from hand skimmed milk. The milk should be kept in a refrigerator or cooler to allow the cream to rise, then carefully hand skimmed.

Adjust the temperature of the milk to 80°F, 26°C.

Add starter. 5 mls per gallon and leave for 40-45 minutes.

Add rennet. 1.5 mls per gallon. Stir thoroughly and leave to form a really firm curd (1-2 hours, but do <u>not</u> allow the whey to rise).

Cut carefully into approximately ½" cubes. Stir for 5 minutes.

Pitch or allow to settle for 15 minutes and then stir again for a further 5 minutes.

Pitch for approximately 1 hour.

Draw the whey and push up the mass of curd.

Cut the curd into blocks about 2" square, bundle in a cloth and put the bundle on the draining rack.

Turn and rebundle the blocks of curd at 10-15 minute

intervals for about 2 hours.

The texture of the curd should by this time be flakey but still moist.

Mill into ³⁄₄" pieces.

Add salt. 1 oz per 2¹⁄₂ lbs curd and mix thoroughly.

Pack into molds lined with damp cheesecloth packing carefully but not pressing down too firmly.

Put to press with light pressure — just enough to cause the whey to run freely.

Next morning turn into a clean, warm, damp cloth. If the cheese is not consolidating properly, dip into water at 140°F, 60°C for 30 seconds before returning to press at medium pressure for a further 24 hours.

On the third day remove the cheese from the press and cloth.

Rub all over with dry salt and put to store.

If a really blue cheese is required, blue mould culture should be added at milling and the cheese may need needling after two weeks in store. This is a slow maturing cheese and will not be ready to use for at least 4 months.

Acidities

At renneting	0.24%
At drawing the whey	1.7
At milling	5.0

Faults in Dorset Cheese

Low fat cheeses are often dry and hard if they are not packed and pressed very carefully.

Cracked rinds can occur in this cheese because the coat is not greased. Correct storage conditions are very important.

Lack of blue veins in a cheese which has had the blue mould culture added is usually due to too hard pressing or a coat which is hard and dry and does not allow the air to penetrate.

DOUBLE GLOUCESTER CHEESE

Adjust the temperature of the milk to 85°F, 29°C.

Add starter. Approximately 50 mls (3+ tablespoons) per gallon and stir in thoroughly. Leave 40-60 minutes to ripen.

Add Annato. (Sufficient to give a straw colour, not red)

approximately 1.5 ml per gallon in 5 times volume of cold water. Stir for 10 minutes.

Add rennet. 1 ml per gallon; stir thoroughly and top stir until coagulation begins. Leave 45-60 minutes until a firm curd has formed.

Cut the curd into really small cubes about ⅛". Cut in both directions with the vertical knife, followed by both directions with the horizontal knife. Stir gently and then cut again in both directions with the vertical knife and one direction with the horizontal knife.

Stir for 10-15 minutes.

Raise the temperature of the curds and whey gradually to 95°F, 35°C taking 50-60 minutes in the process and stirring carefully throughout.

Stir for a further 10-15 minutes.

Pitch for a few minutes and push up the curd to one end of the vat.

Draw the whey.

Cut the mass of curd into 4" blocks and pile to the side of the vat leaving a channel for the whey.

Cut and turn the blocks at 15-20 minute intervals over the following 1½ to 2 hours removing the whey as it accumulates.

Consolidation and draining can be assisted by covering the curd with a board and applying weights. Do not add too much weight, or fat will be lost to the whey.

The texture of the curd should become firm and rather rubbery.

Mill the curd into ½" pieces

Add salt. ¼ oz per lb of curd and mix thoroughly. Leave to stand for 10-15 minutes so that the salt is thoroughly dissolved and stir again.

Pack into molds lined with damp cheesecloth and put to press with medium pressure for 24 hours.

Turn into a clean dry cheesecloth and return to press at maximum pressure for a further 24 hours.

Remove from the press and cloth, grease well with lard, butter or vegetable fat and return to the press for 4 hours at maximum pressure without a cloth, but with a smooth well fitting follower.

Remove from the press and apply a firm support bandage which can be removed after 2-3 days in store.

Put to store turning daily for the first week and twice weekly thereafter. This cheese can be eaten mild at 6 weeks or allowed to mature for up to 6 months.

Acidities

At renneting	0.19 to 0.20%
At cutting	0.13 to 0.14
At pitching	0.16 to 0.18
At milling	0.6 to 0.65

Faults in Double Gloucester Cheese

Uneven colouring due to lumpy starter, to bad mixing of the Annato, or uneven salt distribution.

Weak colour due to adding the Annato to milk which was acid enough to bleach the colour out.

Poor texture due to uneven milling, poor packing, or inadequate pressing.

DUNLOP CHEESE

This Cheddar type cheese is traditionally made from Ayrshire milk.

Adjust the temperature of the milk to 86°F, 30°C.

Add starter. Approximately 50 mls (3+ tablespoons) per gallon and stir in thoroughly. Leave for 1 hour.

Add rennet. 1.5 mls per gallon diluted in 5 times the volume of cold water. Stir well and top stir until coagulation begins. Leave for 40-50 minutes for a firm curd to form.

Cut the curd into pieces about ½". Cut both ways with the vertical knife and one way with the horizontal knife. Stir for 10 minutes.

Raise the temperature of the curds and whey to 98°F, 37°C taking 50-60 minutes in the process and stirring gently throughout.

Continue stirring 10-15 minutes.

Pitch for 20-30 minutes and then push up the curd to one end of the vat.

Draw the whey.

Cut the mass of curd into 4" blocks and pile down the sides of the vat leaving a channel for the whey.

Tear the blocks apart, turn and restack at 20-30 minute intervals over the next 1-1½ hours removing the whey as it accumulates.

The texture of the curd will become smooth and silky and will tear, rather than break.

Mill into ¾" pieces, mix well and leave in a warm place for 5 minutes.

Add salt. 1 oz per 3½ lbs per curd. Mix thoroughly.

Pack into a mold lined with damp, warm cheesecloth. Apply the follower and put to press with minimum pressure for 15 minutes increasing to medium pressure for the next 3 hours.

Turn into a clean damp cheesecloth and return to press at maximum pressure for 24 hours.

Remove from the press and cloth and dip in water at 140°F, 60°C for 30 seconds.

Return to the press in a clean dry cloth for a further 24 hours.

Remove from the press and rub the cheese all over with lard, butter, or vegetable fat. Return to the press without a cloth but with a smooth well fitting follower for 4 hours at maximum pressure.

Put to store turning daily for the first week and twice weekly thereafter.

This is a mild flavoured cheese which can be used from 8 weeks old.

Acidities

At renneting	0.20%
At cutting curd	0.13 to 0.15
At pitching	0.16 to 0.18
At whey drawing	0.23 to 0.25
At milling	0.60 to 0.65

Faults in Dunlop Cheese

Apart from faults common to all cheese caused by unsatisfactory ingredients or poor hygiene, this cheese is subject to the same possible faults of coat as Cheddar and care must be taken in the store.

LANCASHIRE CHEESE

This cheese is made from curd produced on two or even three consecutive days. It is therefore particularly useful when milk is in short supply. The milk should be used raw and can be either from one milking or mixed morning and evening milk provided the milk from the earlier milking has been kept properly cooled.

Adjust the temperature of the milk to 70°F, 21°C.

Add starter. 5-6 mls (one teaspoon) per gallon.

Raise the temperature of the milk to 85°F, 29°C and leave for 40-60 minutes.

Add rennet. 1.5 ml per gallon diluted in 5 times the volume of cold water. Stir well and top stir until coagulation begins. Leave for 40-60 minutes until a firm curd is formed.

Cut the curd both ways with the vertical knife, followed by both ways with the horizontal knife into approximately ¼" cubes.

Drain the whey by pouring the cut curd into a coarse cloth. Bundle the curd up in the cloth and place the bundle on a draining rack.

Leave to drain until the curd is fairly dry and can be handled without breaking. This may take up to an hour.

Cut the curd in to 4" blocks and transfer carefully into a clean coarse cloth in or on the drainer.

Place a board on top of the bundle and add weights to assist the whey to run freely. Do not add too much weight or there will be fat loss to the whey.

The bundle is opened and the curd broken, but not crumbled, by hand into small pieces at fifteen minute intervals, replacing the board after each break and adding weights if necessary to keep the whey running.

Four to six breaks are usually sufficient to produce a curd which is firm but not tough and moist but not wet.

Cut this curd into blocks about 3" square, put in a shallow tin, cover with a moist cloth and leave in a warm place until the following day(s). During this time the acidity of the curd will develop to a point where, when mixed with less matured curd, it gives a suitable average acidity for the finished cheese.

Milling and mixing the curds follows when sufficient curd has been collected, and the final batch has reached the stage where it is ready to leave the drainer.

Transfer all the curd to a large vessel where a temperature of 70-72°F, 21-22°C can be maintained.

Add salt. 1 oz per 3½ lbs curd by sprinkling over the curd blocks.

Mill into pieces approximately ¾".

Mix thoroughly to ensure even distribution of the different curds.

Fill the mixed curds loosely into a mold lined with a warm damp cloth and leave to drain for several hours.

Turn the cheese in the mold over onto a follower to encourage further drainage. The length of drainage time will vary according to the amount of whey in the curd, and to the convenient time to move on to the next stage in the production. As a guide, curd milled and mixed in the morning will be turned over in the evening and put to press the following morning. If the curd is dry, it will be necessary to put to press sooner or the curds will not bond well.

When the curd has drained the cheese is turned into a clean damp cheesecloth, a follower is added and the cheese is lightly pressed for 12 hours.

Turn into a clean cloth and increase to full pressure for a further 12 hours.

At this stage it is often necessary to assist the forming of a smooth coat by dipping the cheese for 30 seconds into water at 140°F, 60°C before returning to press in a clean dry cloth for a further 24 hours at full pressure.

Remove the cheese from the press. Take away the cloth and grease the cheese thoroughly with lard, butter, or vegetable fat.

Return to press at medium pressure without a cloth but with a well fitting flat follower for a further 6-12 hours to give a well shaped cheese.

Put to store, re-greasing if necessary.

Turn daily for the first week and twice weekly thereafter.

This cheese can be used at 4 weeks old. It should have a mild acid flavour and be rather soft to cut. After 8 weeks the flavour becomes more pronounced and the texture smoother

and firmer.
Acidities

At cutting	0.11%		
At draining whey	0.13		
from drainer	0.14		
At fourth break	0.18		
At milling:			
new curd	0.20		
At old curd	1.3	to	1.6
Mixed curds approx.	0.9	to	0.99
	summer		winter

To achive the correct acidity for the mixed curd the proportion of each day's curd can be adjusted, e.g. $^1/_3$ 48 hour curd at 1.6 acidity + $^1/_3$ 24 hour curd at 1.2 acidity + $^1/_3$ new curd at 0.18 acidity = average acidity of 0.99 which is a good winter mix. In summer the average acidity can be reduced by adding a greater proportion of new curd, but it is probably better to use equal proportions of 24 hour curd at 1.6 acidity and new curd at 0.2 acidity to give an average acidity of 0.9

The formula for assesing mixing proportions is as follows:

$$\text{lbs of old curd available} \times \frac{(\text{acidity of old curd} - \text{average acidity required})}{(\text{average acidity required}) - \text{acidity of new curd})}$$

$$= \text{lbs new curd required.}$$

Faults in Lancashire Cheese

Apart from those common to all pressed cheese, caused by faulty ingredients or processes, the main fault with this cheese will be an uneven texture throughout or an uneven coat. This can be caused by the mature curd having become too dry during ripening or by insufficiently thorough mixing of the various curds before packing.

LEICESTER CHEESE (A Red Cheese)

Adjust the temperature of the milk to 70°F, 21°C.
Add starter. 100 mls per gallon (6-7 tablespoons). The starter should be added through a strainer, as small lumps will spoil the even colour of the finished cheese. Stir thoroughly.

Add Annato, approximately 2.5 mls (½ teaspoon) per gallon. Stir thoroughly for several minutes to ensure even distribution.

Raise the temperature of the milk to 85°F, 29°C. Leave for 15 minutes to ripen.

Add rennet. 1.5 mls per gallon in 8 times the volume of cold water. Stir thoroughly and top stir until coagulation begins.

Leave for 40-50 minutes until a firm curd is formed.

Cut the curd both ways with the vertical knife and both ways with the horizontal knife. Stir gently for a few minutes until the curd is floating freely.

Cut again with the vertical knife to give particles ¼" or less, being careful not to crush the curd.

Raise the temperature of the curds and whey to 95°F, 35°C, taking 40 minutes in the process and stirring gently all the time.

The texture of the curd particles should be fairly firm and they should not stick together when gently squeezed in the hand.

Pitch for 5 minutes and then lower a board onto the mass of curd in the whey, adding weights to consolidate the particles. Do not add too much weight or fat will be lost to the whey. Leave for a further 10-20 minutes before drawing the whey.

Cut the curd into blocks about 4" square and pile two deep down the sides of the vat leaving a centre channel for the whey.

Cut, turn and restack the blocks of curd at 15-20 minutes intervals over the next 1½ or 2 hours, removing the whey as it accumulates and keeping the curd warm throughout the process.

The texture of the curd should become smooth and silky and will remain fairly moist.

Mill the curd into pieces about ⅜". Stir the milled curd thoroughly to make sure the particles are even in size and not sticking together.

Add salt. ¾ oz per 4 lbs curd sprinkled evenly over the surface of the curd and mixed in very thoroughly.

Pack into molds lined with damp cheesecloth, apply follower and put to press with light pressure for 6-8 hours.

Turn into a clean damp cheesecloth, return to press for

approximately 12 hours at medium pressure.

Turn into a fine smooth cloth and return to press for 24 hours at increased pressure.

Remove from the press and cloth, grease well with lard, butter, or vegetable fat and return to press, without a cloth, at maximum pressure for 8 hours to give a smooth coat.

Put to store, turning daily for first week and twice weekly thereafter.

This cheese can be used after 4-6 weeks, but will be better if allowed to mature.

At renneting	0.20%
At cutting	0.12 to 0.125
At drawing the whey	0.18 to 0.2
At milling	0.45 to 0.55

Faults in Leicester Cheese

Colour defects which are common in coloured cheeses are caused by insufficient stirring after the addition of the Annato, lumpy or badly mixed starter, uneven salting, or, when accompanied by off flavours or smells, bacterial contamination.

WENSLEYDALE CHEESE

Adjust the temperature of the milk to 70°F, 21°C.

Add starter. 5-7 mls per gallon.

Raise the temperature of the milk to 84°F, 29°C taking about 20 minutes in the process.

Add rennet. 1 ml per gallon in 4 times the volume of cold water. Stir thoroughly and top stir until coagulation begins. Cover and leave to form a firm curd, usually about 40 minutes. Do not allow the milk to get cool during this time.

Cut the curd carefully both ways with the vertical knife. Stir thoroughly and pitch for 10 minutes.

Cut the curd with the horizontal knife until the particles are 1/4-1/2" in size. Be careful not to damage the curd.

Pitch for 20 minutes.

Raise the temperature of the curds and whey to 86°F, 30°C whilst carefully stirring.

Pitch for a further 20 minutes.

Strain the curd into a large coarse cloth.

Remove the curd from the cloth as soon as the whey has drained off.

Cut the mass of curd into 4" blocks and place on a draining rack, covered with a cloth to keep them warm.

Turn the blocks at 15-20 minute intervals over the next 1-1½ hours.

The texture of the curd should become soft and flakey and just moist when squeezed.

Mill into ¾" pieces.

Add salt. ¼ oz per gallon of milk used.

Pack carefully into unlined molds and stand for 2-3 hours.

Turn into moist cloths, return to the mold and leave overnight with followers but without pressure.

Next day turn the cheese into a dry cheesecloth and return to press with medium pressure for 6-8 hours.

Remove from the press and grease thoroughly with lard, butter, or vegetable fat.

A strip of cloth fixed firmly round the sides of the cheese will help it to retain its shape and can be removed after 2-3 days.

Keep for 8 hours in a cool well ventilated place, turning at least once in this period.

Put to store turning daily for the first week and twice weekly thereafter.

This cheese is ready for use from two weeks old but will benefit from a longer maturing period. At 4 weeks it is a mild, slightly acid, cheese, getting richer, sweeter and creamier with age.

If a BLUE WENSLEYDALE is required the blue mould culture should be added to the curd at salting. The curd should be more loosely packed and only light pressure applied. The cheese can be 'needled' during storage to allow air to enter and encourage mould growth.

Acidities

At renneting	0.19%
At cutting	0.14
At pitching	0.16
At drawing whey	0.24 to 0.26
At milling	0.5 to 0.56

Faults in Wensleydale Cheese
Gassy or 'blown' cheese is caused by faulty hygiene, spoilt
milk or contaminated culture.
Misshapen cheese is due to bad storage conditions, infrequent
turning or an inadequate support bandage.

GOAT'S MILK CHEESE

There is no scientific basis for the widely held belief that
goat's milk is resistant to bacterial spoilage and remains
'sweet' for considerable periods of time without protection.
The cheesemaker will be well advised to ignore this theory
and treat the goat's milk with the same care as cow's milk. In
fact a case could be made for taking even greater care with
goat's milk:

Goats are rarely milked under milking parlour
conditions, being frequently milked in the open yard, or at
best in an empty goat stall. They are mostly hand milked into
buckets which are open to the dusty atmosphere and as the
dung of goats is dry, unlike cows', the dust must often be
partly composed of powdered dung pellets containing gut
bacteria. Goat milk for cheesemaking must be carefully
strained and used fresh or cooled and deep frozen within
minutes of leaving the udder. Deep frozen milk will keep for
up to 3 months; it freezes well in polythene bags and can be
thawed far more quickly in these than in any solid container.
The handling and use of frozen milk is not a matter for the
amateur. Experienced professional advice should be sought.
It is unusual and often considered inadvisable to heat treat the
goat's milk for cheesemaking. Like cow's milk, if the milk is
produced under the best possible conditions, it should be
unnecessary to treat it and there is no doubt that raw milk,
straight from the udder, makes the best cheese.

If it is necessary to collect milkings in order to have
enough milk to make cheese, then the milk must be filtered
and cooled efficiently and refrigerated at a temperature
below 43°F, 6°C. It is important to bear in mind that goat's
milk is more susceptible to taints and off flavours than is cow's
milk. The natural diet of the goat is far more varied and
therefore likely to include aromatic and bitter shrubs and

weeds, the flavour of which is passed to the milk. The Billy Goat smell can be transferred to the milk by a careless milker and therefore personal hygiene must be meticulous. Goats often have mastitis of a low infection or subclinical nature and whilst the goat appears fit and milks out normally, the milk may be bitter or salty and the cheese would be flavoured accordingly. There is another condition of the goat udder, reputedly of vitamin deficiency origin, which also gives rise to bitter, off-flavoured milk. The goat milk for cheesemaking must be smelt and tasted before use, and no milk which has even the slightest taint or off flavour must ever be used.

From the cheesemaker's point of view, the important difference between goat milk and cow's milk lies mainly in the amount of fat present and the size of the fat 'globules'. Goat's milk usually contains 4-6% fat which is not very different from high fat, such as Jersey, cow's milk, but it is present in the form of particles or globules many times smaller than those in the milk of cows. This gives the milk a distinctive texture which is sometimes compared with homogenized cow's milk. It also affects the colour of the milk giving a matt white milk which makes opaque white cheese, and as with high fat cow's milk, there is the danger of wasteful fat loss to the whey during processing which is considerably increased by the structure of the fat. The coagulating properties of the milk are also different.

Most cow's milk cheese recipes are totally suitable for goat's milk, and indeed some, such as Wensleydale, have traditionally been made from goat's milk or mixed goat and cow's milk; but the home cheesemaker will need to make certain adjustments to the instructions and recipes to compensate for the structural difference in the milk and to protect the curd against excessive fat loss. Goat's milk requires either twice the amount of standard cheese rennet or twice the length of coagulating time as that given in the instructions for cow's milk in order to give the same strength of curd. The curd must be cut very carefully, stirred very gently to avoid damage and fat loss, and where scalding is recommended, the temperature must be raised slowly and steadily to a point 3.5°F, 2°C lower than that recommended for cow's milk.

It is probably not advisable to use goat's milk to make Cheddar cheese. Cheddar has the lowest water content of all English hard cheese, and as goat's milk cheese tends to be drier than cow's milk cheese anyway, the cheesemaker runs the risk of an over dry wasteful cheese. All the other cheeses, both hard and soft, which are included in this book are excellent and of distinctive flavour when made with goat's milk or a mixture of goat's and cow's milk.

For the benefit of the beginner the following instructions have been adjusted for use with 100% goat or mixed goat/cow milk.

BASIC CURD CHEESE in a mold or a bag

Adjust the temperature of the milk to 90°F, 32°C.

Add starter. 3.5 mls per gallon and stir thoroughly.

Add rennet. 3 mls per gallon diluted in cold water and stir well in. Top stir until coagulation begins. Leave for 3-4 hours until a firm curd has formed.

Either

Ladle in thin even slices into a cloth. Gather up the four corners of the cloth and hang to drain for 12-24 hours before scraping from the cloth into a bowl.

Add salt to taste.

Pack into pots or other containers and keep in a refrigerator for up to 7 days.

Or

Ladle the curd in thin even slices into a mold standing on a mat and board. The mold can be topped up as the curd sinks. Leave to drain until the curd is firm and the mold can be removed without the curd losing shape.

Turn the cheese onto a clean mat and board and leave a further 12 hours.

Lightly salt the cheese on all sides. Wrap in plastic film and store in a refrigerator for up to 7 days.

GOAT MILK CHEESE FOR KEEPING

Adjust the temperature of the milk to 85°F, 29°C.

Add starter. 5 tablespoons, 75 mls per gallon. Stir well and leave for 35 mins.

Add rennet. 2 mls per gallon. Stir thoroughly and top stir for 10 mins. Cover and keep warm until a firm curd has formed, approximately 1 hour.

Cut the curd carefully both ways with the vertical knife and one way with the horizontal knife. Stir very gently, being careful not to damage the curd. Any pieces of curd more than 1/2" diameter can be cut with a sharp knife and returned to the whey.

Raise the temperature of the curd to 90°F, 32°C, taking 30-40 minutes in the process and stirring very gently throughout.

Pitch for 30 minutes.

Draw the whey and push up the curds into a block at one side of the vessel.

Cut the mass of curd into 3" square blocks and stack them at the side of the vessel.

Recut and turn the blocks every 20 minutes for approximately 1 1/2 hours until the curd is flakey and contains very little moisture.

Mill the curd into pieces the size of a small cherry.

Add salt. 1/4 oz per gallon of milk used.

Pack into a mold lined with warm damp cheesecloth and leave unpressed for 2-4 hours.

Turn into a clean damp cheesecloth and return to the mold applying medium pressure for 24 hours.

Turn into a dry muslin and press for a further 2 days turning daily into a clean cloth.

Grease thoroughly with vegetable fat or whey butter and return to the mold without a cloth but with a smooth well fitting follower at medium pressure for 4 hours to ensure a good finish to the coat.

This cheese is ready for use at 4-6 weeks but will keep with advantage for up to 6 months.

The goat's milk cheesemaker who is making cheese for resale is reminded of the following points. One hundred per cent goat's milk cheese is frequently purchased by people with a bovine allergy. It is therefore essential that it is made with powdered starter prepared in goat's milk and not with liquid milk based starter prepared in cow's milk. Vegetarian rennet which is prepared from bacteria should be used unless a supply of kid rennet is available. Do not use the standard cheese rennet prepared from calf stomachs.

The legal requirements both for the preparation and also the resale of cheese as referred to in chapter 5 are, by implication, applicable equally to goat's milk and cow's milk products. Great care must be taken in the labelling of goat cheese, particularly with respect to the fat content of the cheese. The butterfat percentage in raw goat's milk is likely to vary more than it does in cow's milk and therefore the fat content of the cheese is also more variable. The fat loss to the whey is less controllable, particularly in the production of soft goat cheeses, and it is extremely easy to slip from one classification to another, thereby becoming in breach of the regulations.

Mixed milk cheese must be labelled as such or bear a label stating the percentage of cow's milk included.

EWE'S MILK CHEESE

The keeping of ewes for milking is a form of dairying which in years gone by was the most common throughout Britain. However it died out on the introduction of the modern dairy cow and has only recently begun to be reintroduced.

There is no doubt that ewe's milk is economical to produce and that ewe's milk cheese is not only simple to make and delicious to eat but is also a high yield product, and for cheesemakers interested in producing for sale it has a very high retail value.

There is an enormous difference in content and structure between the milk of ewes and that of goats or cows, and although most recipes and instructions for cheese made with other types of milk can be adapted for use with ewe's milk, the cheesemaker should first understand the composition of the milk in order to make the correct adjustments.

Ewe's milk contains almost 10% less water than the milk of either cows or goats, which means a much higher yield of cheese per gallon. Both goat and cow's milk yield about 1 lb cheese per gallon, but a yield of $2\frac{1}{2}$ to 3 lbs per gallon of ewe's milk is not impossible.

The milk also contains approximately 8-9% fat which means that although a full fat rich cheese can be produced with careful handling of the curd, there will still be a considerable amount of fat in the whey, and therefore this is probably the only type of whey which is worth reprocessing at a domestic level. A number of cheese-type products can be produced from ewe cheese whey on its own.

The high fat content of the ewe's milk is present in a form similar to goat's milk. The size of the fat globule being very small compared with cow's milk, and the texture of the milk being white and 'homogenized', this means that the milk can satisfactorily be deep frozen whilst awaiting processing.

The milk sugar or lactose content of the milk is more or less standard for the three types of milk and therefore the lactic acid development during cheesemaking is not very different.

Although the mineral content of the three milks is similar, the protein, particularly the casein content of ewe's milk, is about twice that of either of the others and therefore it is very readily coagulated on renneting.

When adapting a cheese recipe for use with ewe's milk, the following basic rules should be observed.

1. Use good powdered starter prepared either in diluted ewe's milk or mixed goat/ewe milk.

2. Add starter at the standard rate and ripen for the normal period.

3. Add rennet about 3-5 times less than for cow's milk, 6-10 times less than for goat's milk. Top stir carefully and allow approximately the same coagulation time as for cow's milk, although under ideal conditions coagulation may be considerably quicker.

4. Cutting or ladling of the curd must be very carefully done. Ladle in thicker slices or cut to a larger cube size than for either goat or cow's milk cheese. There is considerably less whey to escape from ewe's milk curd and thin slices or small cubes could lead to excessive fat loss and over-dry curd.

5. Use the scald temperature and times recommended for goat's cheese and raise the temperature slowly and evenly. Stir *very* gently.

6. Ewe's milk cheese requires less salt. Use approximately half the amount recommended for other cheeses.

7. Mill the curd to a smaller size and pack firmly and evenly into the mold.

8. Use only light or medium pressure — no ewe's milk cheese needs full pressure.

9. Brining the finished cheese is preferable to greasing or wax coating, and ewe's cheese does not require bandaging or casing.

10. Mature a small (4-6 lb) cheese for up to 6 weeks, but if longer maturing is intended, then the humidity of the storage must be high or the cheese will become hard, dry and very strong in flavour.

The recipes and instructions that follow are either traditional continental recipes adapted for the home cheesemaker or they are cow and goat milk cheeses adjusted for ewe's milk. It is sometimes said that ewe's milk cheese requires no pressing. However, light or medium pressing has been recommended in some of these instructions in order to produce a properly consolidated curd and a good sound coat.

ROQUEFORT TYPE BLUE EWE'S MILK CHEESE

Probably the best known ewe's milk cheese is the Roquefort. This is a creamy, strong, salty blue cheese which can by law only be made in certain areas of France and matured in caves where the conditions are ideal for the growth of the mould. For these reasons the home cheesemaker cannot made a true Roquefort cheese, but a pleasing blue cheese can be made by a similar method. The blue mould culture of Penicillium Roquefortii is the same as is used for Dorset or Stilton and is available from suppliers.

Adjust the temperature of the milk to 90°F, 32°C.

Add rennet. 0.6 ml per gallon. Top stir until coagulation begins. Leave for approximately 2 hours to form a really firm curd.

Cut carefully into 1" cubes being very careful not to damage the curd.

Stir gently in the whey for 15 minutes.

Transfer the curd to a coarse cloth on a drainer and leave to drain, without pressure, until the whey ceases to run.

Break the curd into pieces about 1" diameter and pack quickly in layers into a warm moist mold. Between each layer of curd sprinkle a little blue mould culture prepared according to the manufacturer's instructions. Insert a follower into the mold.

Wrap the mold and cheese in a damp cloth and stand in a cool place.

Turn the curd in the mold at frequent intervals until it slides freely in the mold.

Turn the cheese out onto a board and work up a surface with a knife and hot water.

Coat the cheese liberally with dry salt and put to ripen in a cool, humid place. The ideal ripening conditions for this cheese are a temperature of 46°F, 8°C, with 90-95% humidity. It will be ready for use in 3-5 months and may benefit from 'needling' after the first month if the blue mould is slow to develop.

A HARD EWE'S MILK CHEESE BASED ON CAERPHILLY

Adjust the temperature of the milk to 70°F, 21°C.

Add starter. 75 mls (5 tablespoons) per gallon and leave to ripen for 1 hour.

Raise the temperature of the milk slowly to 88°F, 31°C, taking 30 minutes in the process and stirring all the time.

Add rennet. 0.5 ml per gallon diluted in 10 times the amount of water. Stir thoroughly and top stir until coagulation begins.

Leave for approximately 30 minutes until a firm curd has formed.

Cut the curd carefully in ½" cubes.

Stir gently for 10-15 minutes.

Raise the temperature of the curds and whey to 92°F, 33°C, taking 35-40 minutes in the process and gently stirring throughout.

Pitch for 10-15 minutes.

Push up the curd to one end of the vessel.

Draw the whey quickly from the curd and pile the curd at one end of the vessel in a cone shape.

Leave for 10-15 minutes to consolidate, covered with a cloth to keep warm.

Cut the mass of curd into wedge shaped pieces and stack carefully leaving a channel for the whey to escape. Cover with a cloth and leave for about an hour until a smooth flakey texture is reached.

Mill into pieces about 1" diameter.

Add salt. ¼ oz per 4 gallons milk.

Pack into molds lined with warm moist cheese cloth.

Insert a follower and apply just enough pressure to cause the whey to run. Leave for 2 hours.

Turn out and remold in clean damp cloth.

Apply light pressure for 12 hours.

Remove from the cloth and return to the mold without a cloth and with a smooth follower under medium pressure for a further 12 hours.

Float the cheese for 24 hours in a brine bath. The brine should be made by adding 2 lbs dairy salt or coarse cooking salt to one gallon of boiled water and leaving to cool.

Remove the cheese from the brine, dry carefully on a clean soft cloth.

Leave for 24 hours in a warm well ventilated place to dry and form a firm coat.

Put to store turning daily for the first week and twice weekly thereafter.

This cheese is ready to eat any time after 3 weeks, but will become stronger flavoured as it matures up to about 10 weeks, after which it tends to become dry and hard.

The Pont l'Eveque is the best maturing soft cheese to adapt to ewe's milk, although it is said that a cheese made after the Camembert recipe is interesting although rather dry.

A recipe which is only suitable for use with ewe's milk is based on the simple 'bag curd' cheese. After draining and salting, the curd is formed into small balls and packed in a bowl or jar covered with either olive oil flavoured with herbs or a mixture of oil, rough wine and ground pepper. The length of time that these cheese balls remain in the latter mixture depends entirely on the palate of the consumer.

A CURD CHEESE SUITABLE FOR IMMEDIATE USE

Adjust the temperature of the milk to 90°F, 32°C.

Add rennet. 0.5 ml per gallon diluted in 10 times the quantity of water.

Stir thoroughly and leave to form a firm curd (about 15 minutes).

Ladle into molds on mats and boards or better still, into little baskets.

Leave 12-24 hours to drain.

Lightly salt the surfaces and use immediately or store for a short while in the refrigerator before use to give a firmer cheese.

WHEY

Commercially all whey is recycled. Sometimes it is put through extensive separation equipment in order to reclaim some of the fat and lactose which have escaped the cheesemaking process. The whey butter and milk sugar are used by the confectionary industry. Whey is also dehydrated to produce whey powder for animal feeding and considerable quantities are distributed in the wet state as either feed stuffs or fertiliser.

There are a number of butter and cheese type products which can be made from any type of whey. However the small scale cheesemaker should consider the cost of trying to recover the small amount of food value from the whey from cow or goat's milk with their high water content. The exception to this doubtful economy is the whey from ewe's milk cheese. Not only is the water content very much lower, but there is likely to be at least twice as much fat remaining in the whey. If there is a considerable amount of whey available, then it is worthwhile investing in a home separator and using the product for finishing cheese, for cooking, or blending it with commercially produced butter as an economy measure.

To use up smaller amounts of whey, the most usual

products are 'Ricotta', a whey curd cheese eaten either salted as a cheese spread or with fruit and sugar as a creamy topping, and 'Mysost' which is a chewy, fudgy sweet substance of Norwegian origin.

RICOTTA

The whey is heated to just below boiling point and the white foam which rises to the top is skimmed off and strained through a fine seive or a cloth lined drainer. A higher yield can be produced by adding a pint of whole milk or yogurt to every 3 gallons of whey just before the curds rise.

MYSOST

This is made by boiling the whey continually until only a sticky brown residue remains. This is spooned out hot onto an oiled board and shaped into balls or small cakes. These should be wrapped in plastic film or aluminium foil. Again the yield can be increased by adding whole milk to the whey.

FANCY CHEESES

It has become fashionable in recent years to produce cheese flavoured with beer, wine, herbs, onions, etc. Traditionally the only English cheeses which were made with flavouring were the Sage Derby and the Soft Sage. A cheese was sometimes allowed to mature for a time in a barrel of ale or cyder and there are writings which suggest that port was sometimes poured into a Stilton cheese. This latter practice probably arose from the fact that Stilton made before factory production methods were introduced was usually hard and dry. A hole was drilled in the cheese, and the port, which was poured into this hole, gradually soaked through the cheese, making it soft enough to serve.

It could be argued that a good cheese needs no additional flavouring, the wine, beer, onions, etc. being taken separately at the eater's discretion. However there is public demand for flavoured cheese and therefore the home cheesemaker may well wish to try it.

Cheese flavouring falls roughly into three groups:

1) The addition of flavoured ingredients,

2) A flavouring process during production,

3) Flavour produced during maturing and storage.

The instructions for producing flavoured cheeses which follow include some or all of these processes. They are meant as a guide, not a restrictive list, and the cheesemaker is recommended to experiment until a flavour is achieved which best suits the demand.

ADDED FLAVOUR

Soft and semi-soft cheeses are the most simple cheeses to which flavoured ingredients can be added.

Herbs, chives, etc. are better when used fresh, not dried, and should be well washed, dried, and finely chopped. Use only young leaves and shoots and choose the most colourful. Old herbs tend to be woody and tough and if they are not colourful to begin with, they will look more like bits of dirt than chopped herbs when they appear in the finished cheese. This chopped material can be added between layers of ladled curd or mixed with strained 'bag' curd when it is scraped from the cloth for salting and packing.

Onion or garlic are not easy flavours to balance correctly. Too much will drown the flavour of the cheese; too little gives the impression that the onion or garlic is a taint, rather than a flavour. A freshly crushed clove of garlic rubbed round the bowl in which the 'bag' curd cheese is to be salted is probably sufficient, but by far the easiest way to introduce either of these flavours is by using dried and powdered onion or garlic which can be added with the salt to taste.

Meat or fish. These must be of the highest quality when added, and the cheese containing them must not be kept longer than 4-6 days and must be kept in a refrigerator. It is not advisable to add meat or fish to a ladled cheese as it would be 24 hours at room temperature before the cheese was firm enough to refrigerate, and this is quite long enough for the meat or fish to deteriorate. Small pieces of meat or fish are added to a 'bag' curd at salting and packing. Remember that where salt fish or bacon are added, the amount of salt normally added to the cheese will need to be reduced.

Fruit, etc. Pineapple, raisins, etc. can be added in the

same way as meat or fish. The raisins should be soaked before adding, and the pineapple or other fruits will need to be thoroughly drained.

Hard and semi-hard cheese can have herbs, chives, onion, and garlic added at milling and packing, but it is not advisable to use meat, fish, or fruit with cheese which is to be matured. Commercial manufacturers include pickled onions, nuts, etc. If the home cheesemaker is determined to do this, the onions must be well drained and finely chopped, and the nuts must have their husks removed by dropping them into boiling water for 2 minutes followed by cold water before chopping. The chopping material should be carefully mixed with the milled curd at salting and packing and the finished cheese will need to be kept under careful observation during the maturing period. It would be inadvisable to use a cheese flavoured in this manner if it showed any signs of unnatural development whatsoever.

The introduction of wine to hard cheese is also a somewhat hazardous process for the home cheesemaker. Wine flavouring can be purchased which does not contain live yeasts, but real wine often does, and it is therefore capable of contaminating the cheese in such a manner as to lead to spoilage during maturing. If the cheesemaker is determined to add wine, the wine must be thoroughly boiled and cooled before adding to the curd before packing, or better still the slabs of curd can be marinated in the boiled, cooled wine for a period of one hour before milling, salting, and packing. If the wine flavour is to be enjoyed, the amount of salt should be reduced by about half so that it does not mask the flavour, and the milder more easily maturing types of cheese should be chosen for this sort of flavouring.

FLAVOURING DURING PRODUCTION

If the flavour is to be a part of the cheesemaking process as in the case of marinating or smoking, there are two stages of production at which this can be done. Either the curd can be treated before milling and molding, or the molded cheese can be treated before maturing.

It is obviously not possible to marinate or smoke the

curd for soft cheese until after it has drained and is firm enough to handle. It is safest to leave soft cheese until it is fully drained and molded and then to either lower the cheeses in cloths into the marinating vessel or place them carefully on a mat in the smoking kiln.

Marinating. The soaking of blocks of curd in a suitable flavoured liquid before milling and molding is the best method to use where traces of colour as well as flavour are to be added. The marbled effect of the body of a cheese made from curd marinated in red wine before molding is most attractive, as is the green mottled effect produced by marinating in liquidised herbs in vinegar. Curd blocks soaked in beer or stout will produce a brown marked cheese and cyder sometimes produces an orange or golden mottling. Again the cheesemaker will have to experiment in order to achieve the desired strength of flavour, but blocks of curd rarely need to soak for more than a few hours, and considerably less for the stronger flavours such as vinegar.

Whole cheeses for marinating, such as drained soft cheese or a molded and pressed hard cheese, will not acquire the internal colouring; only the coat and a thin layer inside the coat is likely to undergo any colour change, but careful storage will permit the flavour to penetrate the whole cheese.

Smoking. It is essential to use the cold smoking technique for cheese. At no time must the temperature of the smoke exceed 80°F, 26°C when in contact with the cheese, and over a lengthy smoking 70°F, 21°C is the ideal temperature to aim for. The cheese can either be smoked as blocks of curd before milling, or as whole cheeses. Soft cheese will have to be smoked whole after draining, salting, and molding. Not all cheese is suitable for smoking. The smooth texture, early maturing cheeses, such as the Little Dutch, are ideal. Loose texture hard coated cheeses, such as Cheshire and Wensleydale, are less suitable. It is not recommended to smoke a good Cheddar. The moisture content is already low and the process of smoking could easily produce an over dry cheese. In addition the effect of the smoke on the cheese is likely to retard or even prevent the proper maturing of the cheese during storage.

The whole hard cheese should be put to smoke immediately on removal from the press, before larding or waxing the coat. Smoking is a slow process and the cheesemaker must expect to keep a 4-6 lb cheese in the smoke for at least 36 hours. Only the best hardwood sawdust and chips should be used. Do not use pine or similar as the aromatic oils impart a bitter and unpleasant flavour.

Smoking of small soft cheeses is quicker and simpler. A soft cheese or cheese paté of 8 oz size can be smoked to a quite acceptable flavour in as little as 4 hours. The flavour can be varied by changing the sawdust and wood chip mixture. Try applewood, cherry, or even a small amount of straw or stubble.

FLAVOURING DURING MATURING AND STORAGE

Apart from the aforementioned maturing of cheeses at the bottom of the ale or cyder barrel, there is considerable historical support for the flavouring of cheese by deliberately maturing in a place where aromas and flavours are bound to be picked up. Most obvious of these are the caves that naturally add the blue or white moulds which impart the characteristic flavours of Camembert, Roquefort, and many other famous continental cheeses. The home cheesemaker is advised to avoid self moulding cheeses, but there is no reason why the storage area should not be given an individual aroma by using impregnated timber, such as apple or orange boxes for shelving, etc., provided these have been well cleaned before use.

Individual cheeses can be flavoured by adding the required flavour to the fat or salt which is rubbed into the coat.

A sprig of fresh crushed mint larded onto the coat of a hard cheese will successfully flavour the whole cheese during ripening, as will a similar sprig placed between a curd cheese and its wrapper or under the lid of a cottage or cream cheese pot. The coat of a hard cheese can be rubbed with whisky, brandy, or liqueurs. This will not only flavour the cheese but retard mould growth in store. Cheeses, particularly soft cheeses, wrapped in vine, ash, fern, or nettle leaves during maturing will take up the flavour or aroma of the plant and the rolling of balls of curd, cream, or cottage cheese in oatmeal soaked in fish oil or bacon fat is a very old country habit.

Cheesemakers making for the market will have to take specialist advice before offering a flavoured cheese for sale. The legislation on permissible additives for cheese does not cover any of the aforementioned flavourings other than the sage in Sage Derby. It is possible that the flavoured cheese is covered, not by cheese regulations, but by food regulations referring to cheese products.

PART THREE

AUTHOR'S NOTES, TERMS AND TABLES

AUTHOR'S NOTES

Successful home cheesemakers are likely to find themselves asked to give talks and demonstrations, and also to teach other would-be cheesemakers. Here are a few hints which may prove useful.

Talks. These are usually of short duration, and can be restricted to the cheesemaker's own methods and experiences. The listeners will find it more interesting if it is possible to display a few finished cheeses, preferably with bits to taste. A more useful and ambitious talk on cheesemaking can be prepared by making a cheese at home before the talk and removing a container of the milk, curd, and cheese at each stage of production. If the molded and part pressed cheese can be turned in front of the audience when it has begun to look like 'proper cheese' this can prove most effective. Use a standard type of cheese, such as Cheddar, for this purpose — all the stages of curd preparation are then available. It is a cheese the public recognises, and it is the least likely cheese to be spoilt by the mishandling that may be necessary. Nonetheless you must be prepared to spoil the cheese, and should calculate for this loss in your costings.

Demonstrations at craft displays, agricultural and horticultural shows, etc., are very popular. They can be entertaining, instructive, and very good advertising, but they require careful planning and preparation. These events are usually held in a field under canvas. It is most likely that the demonstrator will be offered a section of an open sided display tent. Obviously this is a far cry from the ideal conditions for cheesemaking. It will be draughty, dusty, and unless the weather is unnaturally kind, not very warm. However, with care, luck, and adjusted techniques, it is possible to make good cheese under these conditions. This summer, at three separate displays, all of them cold and rainy, we managed to produce 8 lbs of Cheddar, which strangely enough grew less mould on the coat than normal, and 4 lbs of Lancashire as good as any we have made at home. The biggest problem is to keep the curd warm during development. Be sure to wrap the vessel well and create a source of hot cloths for covering the curd. A kettle or saucepan full of boiling water with cloths folded on the lid is a good method. Again it is best to try to follow through a known variety of cheese. If time is short, add the starter before the event begins, but keep the interesting and visual stages, such as top stirring, curd cutting, scalding, milling, and molding for doing in front of the crowds. Try to have a good selection of finished cheeses, both soft and hard, on display, and also some commonly used equipment. Duplicated sheets of instructions and names and addresses of suppliers are very useful.

When getting together the equipment to go with you, it is a great help to mentally work through the cheesemaking process putting together the things you would have used as you go along. Do not forget to check that you will be provided with tables sturdy enough to carry the weight of a vessel full of milk and take with you sheets or cloths to cover the tables so that everything looks professional and hygenic.

A Check List for Demonstrators

Tables

Sheets or cloths to cover. Drawing pins, sticky tape, etc.

Trays, mats, boards, etc., for displaying finished cheeses

Lables for varieties of cheese and pieces of equipment

Water

Kettle or similar for heating water

Bowl for washing hands

Towel and soap

Bucket for dirty water

Bucket for used equipment, cloths, etc.

Source of heat, with burner base stable enough for the vessel full of milk

Tea towels

Cheesecloths

Large towel or flannelette sheet or similar for wrapping the vessel in

Milk, starter, rennet, Annato if required, etc.
Vessel
Tablespoon, wooden spoon, ladle
Teaspoon, bowl or cup for rennet, bottle of cold boiled
    water
Knives for curd cutting
Sharp knife for cutting blocks
Bowls and sieves for whey drawing
Bucket for whey collecting
Salt
Molds
Press
Bowl or tray for standing molds on.

It is worth remembering that molded soft cheese will not have drained sufficiently to be safely removed by the time you wish to pack up, so you must either avoid demonstrating coulommier etc., or be prepared to scrap the curd at the end of the day.

Teaching cheesemaking. The most important aspect of cheesemaking classes is the chance for the student to actually 'feel the curd'. However explicit the verbal explanation, the only true way of learning such things as 'clean split coagulation' or top stirring is to do them for oneself, and the difference in the curd at various stages can only be smelt and felt. Therefore the teacher of cheesemaking must be prepared to let the students get their hands in the vat, with the attendant possibility that a less than perfect cheese will result. Make sure that you have calculated for the loss of the cheese in your costings.

The average student of cheesemaking has been influenced by many misguided books and articles which infer that it is either impossible or unrealistically difficult and expensive to make hard cheese anywhere other than under factory conditions. Start your class off optimistically by showing them a good hard pressed cheese which you have made at home. Preferably let them taste it and then let them help to make a similar cheese.

Be prepared to be swamped with questions, particularly

about starters and subculturing. If possible, demonstrate the handling and bottling of starter for freezing, even though it is unlikely that any starter which is subcultured in the presence of a class of eager students will actually be uncontaminated enough to use.

As with talks and demonstrations, if you can arrange to have a cheese in the press for turning or taking out and greasing, this is always appreciated, and if you are teaching Stilton making it is essential that the students get a chance to try 'working up the coat' for themselves.

Be prepared to hand out instructions and notes ready duplicated. Cheesemaking is a craft and your students may well be good at making cheese, but hopeless at taking notes, besides which it is a shame to waste their time and yours writing notes when you could have been handling curd.

THERE ARE a few other things learnt by experience which the new cheesemaker might find useful to know.

The beginner may find that it helps to empty the house of husbands, children, pets, and other distractions until a degree of competence has been reached. An unexpected phone call can lead to over acid curd or over scalding, so perhaps it should be allowed to ring or even be taken off the hook. Once you have gained confidence, you will able to cope with all normal happenings and make good cheese as well.

Remember that perfume, hand cream, hairspray, etc., can be transferred to the milk and therefore to the cheese, as indeed can perfumed soap. Whey tends to 'lift' nail varnish and leave it in the curd, and hairy sweaters somehow always manage to moult into the cheese.

Moulds are everywhere. They are very persistent and fairly resistant to control. The average house will have a reservoir of moulds, sometimes in the very walls of the structure. Do not be surprised if you find that your cheese tends to grow hairy black mould or smooth pink mould instead of the normal white or blue mould. Control this unwanted mould as far as is possible by cleaning everywhere accessible with hypochlorite solution and by fumigating the cheese store. This will probably not clear the trouble up completely, but careful cleaning of the maturing cheeses will mean that it will not spoil the finished article.

When making Stilton, if you are not very proficient at working up a coat, it may help to save one piece of the milled curd at packing, wrap it in plastic film and keep it in the refrigerator. When the cheese is ready to remove from the mold, the spare piece of curd can be mixed to a paste with hot, boiled water and used to make a good coat to the cheese. A rough coated cheese which suffers from cheese mite attack can be rescued if it is caught early. Brush it with a stiff brush and dry salt the coat thoroughly afterwards. Repeat this treatment if the characteristic mite dust reappears.

The fumigation of a mite infested store is a fairly simply matter. Garden stores stock sulphur cones for greenhouse fumigation which are very suitable. Remove all cheese to a safe place first and clean out the dust and debris in the store, preferably with a vacuum cleaner. Cover the ventilation holes in the store if there are any, light the cone, close the door and go a long way away. Do not put the cheese back in the store until several hours after the cone has finished burning, and watch that it hasn't become fly-blown during the time it was out of the store.

Starter again. I make no apology for repeating in detail instructions already given in the earlier part of the book. By far the greatest number of queries I receive refer to the production of good strong starter, and I suspect that most disappointed cheesemakers could trace their difficulties back to their starter.

Many publications suggest making cheese without using a starter at all, or using whey, buttermilk, or commercially produced cheese in the place of starter cultures. Whilst there is no doubt that cheese can be made without starter and that, given time, the natural contaminants will produce the development of lactic acid, this is an unwise and potentially dangerous procedure. At least it could lead to an off-flavoured weak cheese, thereby wasting a considerable quantity of good milk; at worst it could produce a product capable of causing one or another form of food poisoning. The use of whey or buttermilk is to be discouraged for the same basic reasons. There is a high probability that airborne micro-organisms will have settled in the whey or buttermilk, both of which are highly nutritious substances, and they could have become heavily contaminated with undesirable organisms by the time they come to be used in place of commercial starter. The idea that commercial cheese can be used as a source of suitable starter organisms is perhaps the most ill advised and dangerous of all suggestions. By the time cheese reaches the shop it is of indeterminable age; it has been stored and transported under a variety of conditions and handled by a large number of people. It has been displayed, often unwrapped, in a public place and may well have become tainted or contaminated during that time. It is therefore extremely foolhardy to expect to get a suitable culture for making new cheese from such a source. This can only be done by experienced technicians under laboratory conditions and should never be attempted by the home cheesemaker. It is perhaps sensible to mention at this point that the moulds for blue cheese and white coated cheese should never be taken from cheese or bread. Pure mould cultures should be purchased from a reliable source.

Commercially prepared starter is not an expensive item, and it can be made even more economical with proper management.

Liquid Culture.

I personally would not recommend the beginner to use liquid mother culture. In fact I would only use it myself if I were making cheese in sufficient quantity to need to use mixed culture starters on a rotational basis. Most liquid starter culture is more expensive to buy than powdered starter. It is certainly more expensive to pack and post if you are sending for it from a mail order supplier, and it really is much more liable to difficulties in handling. Dried culture is, as it were, at rest, and therefore suffers little or no ill effect from storage and transport, provided the conditions are not too excessive. I am not suggesting that you could expect powdered culture to remain active if it were subjected to very high temperatures, but it will certainly not be affected by any normal climate, provided the packet remains undamaged. Liquid culture is an active living thing. It is affected by temperature within a fairly limited range and too much warmth for any time at all could kill or inactivate a significant number of the bacteria. Some bacteria die or cease to multiply if they are severely shaken whilst in their reproductive cycle, and the length of time that a liquid culture remains in the post might easily be too long for the culture to be at its most active when it arrives. In addition it must be borne in mind that the bacteria have already been handled and therefore exposed to contamination at least once. Although all cultures are produced under careful laboratory conditions, there is far more likelihood of introducing contaminants to your cheese if you are using liquid starter culture. Finally, the only cases of spoiled cheese due to weak or slow starter I have ever come across have belonged to cheesemakers using liquid culture.

Having said all that, there will still be those cheesemakers who want to use liquid cultures. Be extra careful with your cleanliness and sterility and follow the manufacturer's instructions to the letter. Never use a mother culture which is older than recommended, and avoid those which have been a long time in transit.

Dried Culture.

The manufacturer will give the correct instructions for producing your mother culture, i.e. 'Add the packet contents to 1 pint of milk' or 'This sachet will make 1 litre of starter culture'. You must use the whole packet. Once you have opened it the contents cannot be guaranteed to remain unspoiled. Use only fresh, taint-free milk of good quality which is known to contain no residual antibiotics. Bring the milk to the boil, remove from the heat and pour immediately into a clean 'sterile' container with a well fitting lid (I find ½ gallon ice-cream containers ideal), replace the lid and quickly cool the milk to approximately 88°F, 31°C by placing the container in cold water. The temperature can be tested with a thermometer, of course, but after a while you will be able to judge, quite accurately, when the milk is at the correct temperature by feeling the outside of the plastic container. This means one less occasion when the milk must be exposed to the air! Empty the packet of culture powder into the cooled milk and stir with a metal spoon which has been boiled. Replace the lid firmly and put the container of milk into a warm place, such as beside the stove or in the airing cupboard. The ideal temperature is 88°F, 31°C.

Storing of Mother Culture

In order to economise on purchased commercial cultures, it is sensible to divide the mother culture into smaller quantities and to freeze these for later use. If the instructions with the packet of powder give a maturing time, i.e. 'leave for 24 hours', then you should allow about half the recommended period. If no time is stated, then 8-12 hours after making up, the mother culture is usually ready for division. It should look and smell like sour milk, but it is better if rebottled before it becomes solid and lumpy. It should never be allowed to mature for the full recommended time if it is to be frozen for future use. Bacteria which have been allowed to develop in the milk for 24 hours are no longer at peak reproductivity and are not as virile as they were. The systemic shock of freezing may therefore kill a greater percentage of the organisms, thereby weakening the starter, and in the case of a mixed culture it could alter the careful balance between the different bacterial strains.

Fifteen mls (a tablespoonful) of active mother culture from the freezer is ample to prepare a pint of starter. Work out the amount of starter you usually need per batch of cheese and from this choose bottles of the right size in which to store you inoculem. Sterlise your storage bottles, vessels, and utensils very carefully. Contaminated starter is not only wasteful, it could be harmful.

Transfer the semi-mature mother culture to the storage bottles as quickly as possible. The shorter the time the lids are off both bottles and culture container, the less opportunity for contamination. Working beside a lighted gas or a source of steam reduces the changes of airborne contamination but is often inconvenient. A dust and microbe 'tent' can be produced by working in a well-cleaned sink with a large cheesecloth which has been wrung out in weak hypochlorite solution attached to the taps at the back and weighted along the sides of the sink to create a sort of 'roof' over the area in which you will work. Be careful not to let hypochlorite get into the starter.

When the mother culture is safely in the storage bottles, replace the caps and thoroughly clean the outside of the bottles before putting them into the deepfreeze. Holes bored in a piece of polystyrene packing material make excellent stands to keep the bottles upright in the freezer.

Any mother culture left after bottling up can be used to make cheese if the container is resealed and starter left to mature for the remainder of the recommended time.

Subculturing

The preparation of cheese 'starter' from a stored mother culture added to fresh boiled milk is a 'subculture'. Twenty-four hours before cheesemaking, sufficient mother culture should be removed from the freezer and put in a suitable place to thaw. Remember 15 mls of mother culture will make a pint of starter and a pint of starter is generally enough for up to 8 gallons of milk. The length of thawing time will depend on the quantity in each container, but it can be hurried up by putting the sealed containers in cool water. Do not use hot water. This is bad for the starter and can cause the containers to break or split. Once thawed, the mother culture should be added to the appropriate quantity of milk which has been boiled and cooled in the same way as for producing the mother culture. I try to fetch a pint or so of fresh raw milk in which to make up my starter from the same source as the milk for my cheese will come from the following day. This is not always convenient, and I have had no difficulty in using shop bought pasteurised milk for starter, although I wouldn't really recommend it for home cheesemaking. The maturing starter should be covered with a cloth over the vessel to prevent flies from settling on the lid.

This subculture should never be used to make further supplies of starter. Only mother culture is suitable. Excess starter can be drained through a cloth and used as lactic cheese, but if you have calculated carefully there will be too little left over to worry about. Never economise by using old, weak, or poor quality starter. If there is any doubt in your mind at all, do not use it; it is a tragedy to spoil several gallons of milk for the sake of a few pennyworth of fresh starter.

Acidity. The measure of lactic acid present in the milk or whey.

Acid meter. A device for measuring acidity based on the acid/alkali neutralising factor.

Albumin. The milk protein which is heat sensitive.

Alkaline. The alkaline solution used in an acid meter is sodium hydroxide.

Annato. Yellow vegetable colouring especially produced for the dairy industry.

Antibiotics. Pharmaceutical substances that inhibit bacterial growth.

Antiseptic. Chemical substances for reducing bacterial action.

Bacteria. Microscopic life form smaller than fungi and larger than viruses.

Bandages. Strips of loose weave cotton gauze for wrapping round new cheeses.

Brine. A solution of dairy salt in water in which cheese is soaked.

Coat. (See skin or rind). The outer skin of a cheese.

Caps. Rounds of cotton gauze for the tops and bottoms of new cheese.

Carbohydrates. Sugars, starches, cellulose, mucilage, and gum.

Casein. The milk protein which coagulates by the action of acid or enzymes.

Cheese spread. A commercial product made from low grade cheese and emulsifiers.

Chlorine. The active component of sodium hypochlorite.

Coagulate. To come together or thicken. A process brought about by enzyme action.

Coagulum. The solid product of coagulation.

Colostrum. A substance found in the milk of freshly calved cows.

Condensed milk. Milk from which a percentage of the water has been removed.

Contaminant. Unwanted micro-organisms in the milk or cheese.

Culture. A deliberate production of micro-organisms.

Curd. The semi solid product of protein coagulation. That part of the coagulated milk which is not whey.

Curdle. To cause the proteins in the milk to solidify in an irregular manner.

Dry matter. That part of the milk or cheese which is not water.

Emulsion. A mixture of fat and liquid, sometimes incorporating other solids, which does not separate on standing.

Enzymes. Natural products of living things which have a variety of actions including the ability to solidify protein.

Finish. The quality of the coat or rind of cheese.

Finishing plate. A smooth well fitting follower for the final press.

Flora. The natural micro-organisms in any environment.

Follower. A disc to place over the curd before applying the press plate.

Fumigate. To cause the cleaning of an area by filling it with gases unacceptable to microbes, etc. Burning sulphur is a suitable method to use in a cheese store.

Globule. The spherical fat particles found in milk, the size of which varies from beast to beast.

Heat treatment. The destruction of contaminating organisms in milk by raising the temperature beyond that generally tolerated (see pasteurisation).

Hoops. A term sometimes used for soft cheese molds.

Humidity. The percentage of water vapour in the atmosphere.

Hypochlorite. See sodium hypochlorite.

Incubate. To keep a bacterial culture at optimum temperature to encourage reproduction.

Inoculate. To introduce a bacterial culture into otherwise sterile material.

Inoculem. The culture of bacteria for introduction as above.

Lactic acid. The acid produced by bacterial action on lactose.

Lactose. The sugar present in milk.

Litre. 1000 mls — approximately 4.6 litres to the gallon.

Mastitis. Inflammation of the udder.

Mature. Ripe or to ripen cheese. To keep whilst flavour develops.

Maturing. The process of keeping to advance flavour

development.

Microbes. Moulds, yeasts, bacteria, viruses, etc.

Micro-organisms. Any organism not visible to the naked eye.

Milk solids. All that part of milk which is not water.

Mill. A machine for chopping or tearing cheese curd.

Milling. Reducing the mass of curd to small particles suitable for packing.

Millilitre. Signified ml, also sometimes c.c. or cm^3 = $1/1000$ of a litre.

Minerals. Inorganic matter originally derived from the soil. The chief mineral in milk is calcium.

Mites. Tiny beetle-like creatures which can inhabit cheese stores and attack the surface of the cheese.

M.M.B. Milk Marketing Board.

Molds. In this book MOLD refers to the former, chessell, or hoop in which cheese is packed, and <u>not</u> to the micro-organism.

Mother culture. The original bacterial culture from which other cultures are made.

Moulds. In this book MOULD refers to the micro-organism, not to the vessel in which cheese is packed.

Needling. Piercing the body of a cheese which is to be a 'blue cheese' to allow air to enter and encourage the growth of blue mould.

Organisms. Microbes.

Pasteurise. To destroy most of the organisms present in milk by heat treatment for a short time or at a slightly lower temperature for a longer time.

Pathogenic. Those micro-organisms capable of being injurious to health.

'phage. (Bacteriophage). A condition from which bacteria suffer which alters the structure and activity of the organism.

Pipette. A graduated glass tube for measuring small amounts of liquid.

Pitch. To allow the curd to settle in the whey.

Processed cheese. Reconstituted substandard cheese.

Propagate. To encourage growth, i.e. starter propagation to encourage the reproduction of starter bacteria.

Protein. Complex chemical compounds which are a part of the structure of all living things. The primary milk proteins are casein and albumin.

Purified chalk. A chalk preparation for culinary use available from chemists and homebrewing suppliers.

Random bacteria. Unidentified organisms found in the atmosphere.

Raw milk. Milk which has not been heat treated or adulterated since leaving the udder.

Rennin. The enzyme found in the stomachs of suckling mammals.

Rennet. A preparation of rennin or similar enzyme for clotting or coagulating milk for cheese or junket.

Rice flour. Fine rice starch available from delicatessens.

Rind. The 'coat', 'skin' or outer surface of a cheese.

Ripen (of cheese). To mature and allow the flavour to develop.

Ripen (of milk). To allow time for bacterial reproduction after the addition of the starter.

Ropey (see stringy). Milk containing lumps and threads of solidified protein caused by bacterial action in an infected udder.

Scald. To raise the temperature of the curds and whey, sometimes incorrectly referred to as 'cooking the curd'.

Separated milk. Milk from which some or all of the cream has been mechanically removed.

Separator. A machine for separating the milk from the cream by centrifugal force.

Skimmed milk. Milk from which some of the cream has been removed by hand using a ladle or skimmer.

Sodium hydroxide (NaOH). The alkali used in an acid meter to calculate the amount of lactic acid in the milk or whey.

Solidify. To cause a liquid to take up a 'solid' structure.

Solids not fat. (S.N.F.) That part of the milk which is not fat and is not water.

Sour (milk). Milk in which bacterial action has produced lactic acid causing it to become 'sour', not 'sweet'.

Spoiled milk. Containing contaminants.

Spore. A seed like structure which is part of the reproductive system of some micro-organisms.

Sterile. The absence of microbial contamination.

Streptococcus. A family of bacteria some branches of which are used in cheese starter cultures.

Stringy (see ropey). Threads or strings of protein are found in the milk of a beast with mastitis.

Subculture. A second production of bacteria using the original or mother culture as inoculem.

Sweet (milk). Milk in which no bacterial action to convert lactose to lactic acid has taken place.

Taint. Any smell or flavour transferred from its source to the milk.

Vat. The container in which cheese is made.

Vessel. Any container or holding utensil.

Vitamins. Vitamin A and Riboflavin are present in milk and cheese. 2 oz of cheese can provide the average man with about $1/3$ his daily requirement of vitamin A and $1/6$ his requirement of riboflavin.

Whey. The fluid part of the milk which remains after the coagulation and drainage process.

Whey butter. The milk fat which remains in the whey from cheesemaking can be mechanically separated and used in manufacturing processes.

Whey powder. The remaining water can be evaporated from the whey and the residual powder used for stock feedstuffs.

Yeasts. Large micro-organisms which produce the gas that causes blown cheeses, and usually has a characteristic smell. Used extensively in baking and brewing and found naturally in the 'bloom' on fruit.

COMPARATIVE MEASURES

The following measures are only approximate, but they are sufficiently accurate for cheesemaking.

1 gallon	= 4.546 litres (5 litres approx.)
1 litre	= 1000 ml = 1.75 pints
1 pint	= 20 fl oz
1 fl oz	= 28.5 mls = 8 drams
1 tablespoon	= 15 mls
1 teaspoon	= 5 mls or 3.5 mls
1 dram	= 3.5 mls = 60 minims or drops
1%	= 1 ml in 100 mls or 10 mls per litre = 50 ml per gallon approximately.

Temperature conversion
°F to °C — subtract 32, multiply by 5 and divide by 9
°C to °F — multiply by 9, divide by 5 and add 32.

USEFUL ADDRESSES

Name and Address	Telephone No	Range of equipment
A. G. Ash Millhayes, Stockland Honiton, Devon EX14 9DB	040 488 529	1 lb and 5 lb mold and press. Other molds and formers. Curd knives, 10" standard, others made to order
W. H. Boddington & Co Ltd Horsmonden Kent	089 272 2277	Range of plastic molds, hoops and formers.
Astell Hearson 172 Brownhill Road Catford, S.E.2	01 697 8811	Acid meters, thermometers, Milk and dairy testing equipment. Chemicals
R. J. Fulwood & Bland Ltd Ellesmere, Salop SY12 9DG	01691 069 171 2391	Range of equipment both commercial and small scale. Lists on application.
Christian Hansen 　Laboratories Ltd 476 Basingstoke Road Reading RG2 0QL	01 0734 861 056	Starter cultures. Rennet, Annato, wax, special cultures for blue and moulded cheeses. List available.
Small Scale Supplies Widdington Saffron Waldon, Essex	0799 40 922	Good range of small scale equipment. List on application.
Smallholding Supplies The Old Palace Priory Road Wells, Somerset	074972 127	Wide range of equipment of all types. Own design press. Catalogue (for which there is a charge) on application.
Wheeler Engineers Hoppins Dunchideock Exeter, Devon	993 832238	'Wheeler' press and some other equipment. Also stocked in other outlets.

USEFUL TEMPERATURES FOR CHEESEMAKERS WITH APPROXIMATE CONVERSIONS.

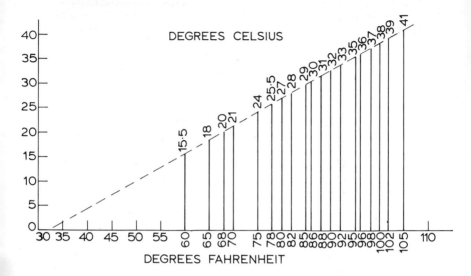